# The Aesthetics
# of Landscape

To my parents
Barbara Anne Randolph Trent
and
Richard George Bourassa

# The Aesthetics
# of Landscape

Steven C. Bourassa

**Belhaven Press**
London and New York

First published in Great Britain in 1991 by
Belhaven Press (a division of Pinter Publishers),
25 Floral Street, London WC2E 9DS

**British Library Cataloguing in Publication Data**
A CIP catalogue record for this book is available from the
British Library

ISBN 1 85293 071 3

For enquiries in North America please contact
PO Box 197, Irvington, NY 10533

**Library of Congress Cataloging in Publication Data**
A CIP catalog record for this book is available
from the Library of Congress

Typeset by Mayhew Typesetting, Bristol, England
Printed and bound in Great Britain by Biddles Ltd of Guildford and Kings Lynn

*Esthetics is often considered a kind of froth, difficult to analyze, easy to blow away. Our culture thinks of sensed form as a surface phenomenon, a luster applied after the inner essence of something is formed. But surfaces are connected to interiors. They play a key role in the functioning of the whole, since the surface is where any interchange goes on. All that we know and feel, beyond our genetic inheritance, comes to us from surfaces.*

Kevin Lynch, *Managing the Sense of a Region* (1976), p. 68.

# CONTENTS

# LIST OF PLATES

# LIST OF TABLES

# PREFACE

In the *Phaedo* (Plato, 1969), which relates the events of the day of his execution, Socrates discussed the cause of beauty in objects: 'it is safe for me or for anyone else to answer that it is by Beauty that beautiful things are beautiful' (p. 159). As his last words on the subject, this statement might seem to imply that Socrates had become extremely pessimistic about the ability of philosophy to say anything meaningful about aesthetics. One can only imagine what Socrates would have thought if he had become familiar with the subsequent history of philosophical ideas on aesthetics - what Scruton, in his *The aesthetics of architecture* (1979), referred to as a 'continuing intellectual disaster' (p. 202). In view of the apparent ongoing substantiation of Socrates' early pessimism, one would have to be foolish, or at best audacious, to embark on yet another attempt to say something meaningful - not to mention interesting - about aesthetics. As Passmore (1967) put it, 'if books on aesthetics do not quite take the prize for dreariness, at least they stand very high on the list' (p. 36).

On closer reading, however, it becomes evident that Socrates' comment is more ironic than pessimistic. 'Beauty' here refers to the Form of Beauty, or absolute beauty, which we might characterize as the theory of beauty. In other words, Socrates was saying that before one can properly claim that an object is beautiful, one must comprehend the meaning of beauty. Although aesthetics is not concerned only, or even primarily, with beauty (Dewey, 1934; Passmore, 1967), Socrates' statement could be extrapolated readily into a forceful argument in support of the development of theory in aesthetics. Furthermore, the history of aesthetic ideas gives cause for more sanguinity than Scruton allows. While perhaps no single theory is entirely convincing, there is some truth in aspects of various theories. In the chapters that follow, those theories will be called upon frequently to shed light on the subject of landscape aesthetics.

One of the more important points made in the following chapters is that aesthetic values must be viewed in their cultural and historical contexts. Thus, in Chapter 2, I reject Kant's notion of the 'universal subjectivity' of aesthetic judgment, and part of Chapter 5 is devoted to a consideration of the aesthetic values maintained by different cultural groups. Just as aesthetic values need to be viewed in their cultural contexts, so must aesthetic theories. Theories of aesthetics are sometimes advanced in support of a specific, often new, set of cultural values. For example, the formalist theory of Bell and Fry (see Chapter 2) was clearly an attempt to legitimate a particular artistic style - in this case, non-representational painting. But to argue, as Weitz (1956) did, that aesthetic theory must necessarily be limited to some such *advocacy* role, is to be unduly skeptical about its potential *explanatory* role. Aesthetic theory can be explanatory in at least three important ways. First, if, as some theorists claim, aesthetics has a biological basis, then there may be some universal principles of aesthetics (see Chapter 4). Secondly, it is possible to make some useful general observations about the cultural basis for aesthetics, observations which do not depend on the values of particular cultures (see Chapter 5). Thirdly, it is possible to make some meaningful theoretical statements about the ways in which cultural values are changed (see Chapter 6).

Of course, all theory - whether aesthetic or otherwise - is to some extent culturally determined. The pages that follow are certainly a product of their time, reflecting issues and questions raised in the recent literature in landscape aesthetics and related fields. It is hoped, however, that the ideas presented here go beyond mere advocacy of a particular style - although, as someone is certain to point out, I do make some specific stylistic recommendations in Chapter 8 - and help to clarify some of the more general theoretical issues in landscape aesthetics.

Among those who have investigated the matter, there is a clear consensus that theory has been neglected in landscape aesthetics (Basch, 1972; Appleton, 1975b; Carter, 1976; Wohlwill, 1976; Penning-Rowsell, 1981; Porteous, 1982b; Punter, 1982; Zube et al., 1982; Priestley, 1983; Sell et al., 1984; Sancar, 1985; Eaton, 1989). There has been a vast amount of research in the field, but that research has not been unified or informed by any comprehensive theory of landscape aesthetics. Instead, the various research efforts are either atheoretical or reflect fragmented and apparently incompatible theoretical bases. A salient example is the fact that much of the fairly voluminous published work in landscape evaluation lacks any coherent foundation in aesthetic theory. As Zube et al. (1982) noted: 'Research without a general theory is fragmentary and has a hit-or-miss quality to it; it is hard to understand how various research efforts fit together, or indeed, if they are measuring the same thing' (p. 25). The work that has been done on theory tends to focus exclusively on either biological or cultural bases for aesthetic behavior, without any attempt to reconcile those apparently incompatible sets of explanations. Exceptions to this include papers by Zube (1984) and Dearden (1989) and a recent book by R. Kaplan and S. Kaplan (1989), all of which emphasized the need to consider both biological and cultural aspects of landscape aesthetics; these works do not, however, address the theoretical issues which divide the biological and cultural camps. Priestley (1983) observed aptly that the field of landscape aesthetics lacks a 'paradigm'. Using Kuhn's (1970) terminology, Priestley claimed that the field is in a 'pre-paradigm period' and that its primary need is paradigm development.

The central purpose of this book is to present a paradigm for research in landscape aesthetics. This book is in large part a response to Appleton's *The experience of landscape* (1975a), which was the first attempt to develop a comprehensive theory of landscape aesthetics. While there were previous theories of aesthetics which addressed the question of landscape, Appleton's book must be viewed as the first to focus exclusively on landscape as an aesthetic object. To the extent that my book is a response to Appleton's work, I owe a great debt to Appleton for his willingness to pioneer in what was and continues to be a highly speculative - and excruciatingly interdisciplinary - area of research. Nevertheless, I will not hesitate to point out the significant shortcomings in Appleton's thesis.

One of the major shortcomings of Appleton's book was its failure to address adequately the history of ideas about aesthetics and landscape. In response to those lacunae, this book commences with two philosophical chapters which deal respectively with the meanings of the two key concepts of 'landscape' and 'aesthetics'. Chapter 1 is concerned with the nature of landscape as aesthetic object. I observe that landscape is a particularly unwieldy aesthetic object. It is a messy mix of art, artifact and nature, and it is inextricably intertwined with our everyday, practical lives. The intractable landscape refuses to conform to the neat philosophical model of aesthetic objects as discrete works of fine art that are somehow set apart from mundane existence. It is perhaps no wonder that philosophers have displayed a rather agoraphobic avoidance of the landscape. I conclude Chapter 1 with a review of the parallels between architecture and landscape as aesthetic objects. Landscape, like architecture, demands an aesthetics of everyday experience - that is, an aesthetics of engagement rather than the philosophers' aesthetics of detachment.

Chapter 2 proceeds with an analysis of the nature of aesthetic experience. I note that Santayana divided the subject of aesthetics into three levels – sensory, formal and symbolic. After a brief consideration of sensory aesthetics, I discuss some of the conceptual problems of formal theory. I then point out that the idea of symbolic aesthetics helps one to explain the ambiguities in the idea of landscape as well as the conflict between Kant's aesthetics of detachment and Dewey's aesthetics of engagement. This leads to a review of the history of aesthetic ideas concerning the contradiction between the apparent 'disinterestedness' of aesthetic experience, on the one hand, and the concept that the aesthetic is an intensification and enhancement of everyday experience, on the other. I show that the latter argument is the only tenable one for landscape aesthetics. The aesthetics of landscape is a matter of the experience of landscape or, in other words, the interaction of subject and object. Thus theories based purely on either the objective landscape or the subjective perceiver are inadequate.

Having explicated the basic concepts of landscape and aesthetics in Chapters 1 and 2, it then becomes possible to articulate a paradigm for theory and research in landscape aesthetics. A second major shortcoming of Appleton's *The experience of landscape* is its narrowly biological approach to aesthetics. Thus Chapter 3 sets forth a tripartite framework of biological, cultural and personal modes of aesthetic experience as a fundamental organization of the subject of landscape aesthetics. This paradigm is based in part on Vygotsky's developmental approach to understanding the human mind and human behavior. Vygotsky's developmental method leads to the identification of three fundamental processes of development: genetic evolution, cultural history and individual development. These correspond to three modes of existence – the *Umwelt*, *Mitwelt* and *Eigenwelt* – identified phenomenologically by existential analysts. These in turn correspond to three modes of aesthetic experience. The three modes can be characterized as sets of aesthetic constraints and opportunities, labeled *laws*, *rules* and *strategies*, respectively.

Chapters 4 to 6 deal successively with biological laws, cultural rules and personal strategies. Chapter 4 addresses the relationship between survival and aesthetics and the possible connections between early human habitats and modern landscape preferences. In this context, particular attention is given to Appleton's (1975a) prospect-refuge theory of aesthetics. Two other biologically-based theories of landscape aesthetics – information-processing theory and Gestalt theory – are also reviewed. Chapter 5 explores the general characteristics of culture and their manifestations in cultural attitudes to landscape. Stability and identity are stressed as fundamental features of cultural attitudes and rules. I review the literature on variations in the aesthetic attitudes of different groups and suggest a preliminary typology for such attitudes. Then Chapter 6 addresses the personal mode of aesthetic experience, with particular emphasis on the significance of personal creativity as the source of cultural change.

Chapters 7 and 8 demonstrate some applications of the ideas advanced in previous chapters to problems of landscape evaluation and design. Chapter 7 includes critiques of several quantitative evaluation methods of varying degrees of sophistication and offers *landscape criticism* as a model for the evaluation of landscapes. Chapter 8 addresses the topic of landscape design by means of a case study of postmodernism in architecture and planning. The aesthetic theory presented in Chapters 1 to 6 is shown to support the branch of postmodernism called *critical regionalism* by its proponents. I conclude that critical regionalism has the potential to be a significant positive force in shaping the human landscape.

# ACKNOWLEDGEMENTS

In writing this book, I have incurred a debt to numerous individuals, but particularly to Max Neutze and Pat Troy of the Australian National University. Each served as Head of the Urban Research Unit (now 'Program') while I was a postdoctoral fellow there in 1989. Both Max and Pat encouraged me to pursue this book in spite of the fact that I had previously proposed to do something quite different, involving a topic 'miles away' (to use Pat's words) from the subject of landscape aesthetics. I am also grateful to Pat for making available the travel grants which enabled me to see firsthand most of the paintings reproduced in the following pages.

Several other individuals at the ANU or elsewhere in Canberra were especially helpful. Tim Bonyhady, Penelope Hanley, Clem Lloyd, Philip Pettit and Shelley Schreiner of the ANU all provided helpful information and assistance of various sorts. Clem's amusing repartee at tea each morning and afternoon was a particularly welcome antidote to the tedium of sifting through the sometimes 'dreary' (to borrow Passmore's adjective) history of aesthetic ideas. I am also grateful to Chris Hamnett of the Open University, who read Chapter 3 while a Visiting Fellow at the ANU. Although I made a number of revisions to that chapter at his suggestion, I suspect he would still hesitate to endorse the result.

Both Judith Brine and Nino Bellantonio of the University of Canberra provided a number of helpful comments in response to drafts of Chapters 1 to 3. I am also grateful to John Thompson of the National Library of Australia, who commented on those same chapters.

Several individuals at Memphis State University provided invaluable assistance. Tom Wofford of the MSU Photographic Services Laboratory performed the painstaking task of preparing the illustrations for publication. Zurina Bt. A. Hamid, Steven Jacobs and John Johnson all provided helpful research assistance while they were students in the Graduate Program in City and Regional Planning.

I would like to thank the following institutions and individuals who gave permission to reproduce the illustrations: Aboriginal Artists Agency Ltd (Plate 1); Art Gallery of New South Wales (Plates 5 and 9); Australian National Gallery (Plates 13, 17, and 23); City of Ballaarat Fine Art Gallery (Plate 11); Basil Blackwell (Plates 15 and 16); Alan Bond Collection (Plate 25); Paul Delprat (Plate 21); Lady Maisie Drysdale (Plates 7 and 27); Edward Heffernan (Plate 3); Sali Herman (Plate 26); David Moore (Plate 24); National Gallery of Victoria, Melbourne (Plates 19, 22, and 28); National Library of Australia (Plates 6, 18, and 20); Powell Street Galleries, South Yarra (Plate 12); Queen Victoria Museum and Art Gallery, Launceston (Plate 8); William Robinson (Plate 14); Robert A.M. Stern Architects (Plate 29); Margaret A. Streeton (Plate 10); and Warrnambool Art Gallery (Plates 2 and 4).

Much of the material presented in Chapters 3 and 8 appeared in similar form in *Environment and Behavior* (Bourassa, 1990) and the *Journal of Architectural and Planning Research* (Bourassa, 1989). That material is reproduced here with the permission of the publishers of those journals, Sage and Locke Science Publishers, respectively.

Finally, I wish to express my gratitude to Professor Edmunds V. Bunkśe, of the University of Delaware, who first sparked my interest in landscape aesthetics in 1976 in a seminar on culture and the environment. One of my assignments in that seminar was to do a review of Jay Appleton's *The experience of landscape*. I have continued to be preoccupied with some of the issues raised by Appleton's book and the following pages are in essence another, more thorough, attempt to respond to Professor Bunkśe's assignment.

# CHAPTER 1
# LANDSCAPE AS AESTHETIC OBJECT

A scholar's initial exploration of a topic is often incited by an intriguing but rather naively defined problem. Sometimes research leads to the discovery that the problem must be redefined or even abandoned. At other times, it is found that the problem is defined appropriately, but is much more complex than anticipated. As one delves into a problem and comes to appreciate its complexities, one's preliminary understanding of the issue can undergo a complete metamorphosis. What seemed a simple, straightforward question becomes manifestly difficult and imprecise. This is certainly the case with landscape aesthetics. For example, the problem of landscape aesthetics could be defined initially as 'What do we like about landscape and why do we like it?' (Appleton, 1975a, p. vii). But what exactly is *landscape*? And is it adequate to assume that *aesthetics* is concerned with 'what we like'?

These questions are meant to suggest that any study of landscape aesthetics should address basic philosophical questions about the nature of the subject matter. Langer (1953) observed that the focus of philosophy is on the meanings of what we say. Scruton (1979) echoed this by noting: 'Philosophy . . . attempts to give the most general description possible of the phenomena to which it is applied. Such a description tells us, quite simply, what we are talking about when we refer to something' (p. 2). The two most fundamental questions in landscape aesthetics involve the meanings of landscape and aesthetics. Consequently, one of the fundamental inadequacies of Appleton's formulation of the problem of landscape aesthetics - and his solution to the problem - stems from his failure to subject these two basic concepts to philosophical scrutiny. In fact, Appleton (1975a) essentially dispensed with most of the philosophical literature on aesthetics without addressing many of the salient issues in aesthetics that are quite relevant to landscape.

To attempt to make up for Appleton's oversight, the first two chapters of this book are devoted to the philosophical explication of the concepts of landscape and aesthetics. To some extent, these two concepts must be considered simultaneously because each qualifies the other. Landscape as aesthetic object may be different from landscape generally and, perhaps more importantly, the aesthetics of landscape is not necessarily the same as the aesthetics of other objects. For convenience, however, I shall be exploring the two concepts more or less sequentially, focusing on the idea of landscape in this chapter and saving discussion of the nature of aesthetics for the next.

## The Idea of Landscape

The use of the term *landscape* in this book reflects a traditional focus on landscape in the field of geography. Cosgrove (1984; *cf.* Gold, 1980) has provided an excellent account of the history of the geographical idea of landscape, so I shall mention only some salient points here. Landscape was used initially by geographers such as Sauer to refer to the particular object of study of geography. Writing in the 1920s, Sauer (1963) defined geography as 'the morphology of landscape' and he defined landscape as 'an area made up of a distinct association of forms, both physical and cultural' (p. 321). For Sauer, landscape was more or less synonymous with area or region, and was essentially an object for positive scientific investigation. While he noted that the best geographers – such as von Humboldt (see Bunkśe, 1981) – did not ignore the aesthetic qualities of landscape, it is clear that Sauer did not envision geography as embracing the systematic study of landscape aesthetics.

Contemporary geographers rarely use the word landscape in the sense in which Sauer employed it. Terms such as *region, area* and *environment* have largely replaced landscape as the stated objects of scientific geographical study. Indeed, the synthetic branch of geography which seeks to bring together all the various physical and cultural subfields in the subject is referred to as *regional* geography rather than *landscape* geography. Landscape has, however, been adopted recently by the subfield of geography known as humanistic geography (Tuan, 1976a), which is concerned essentially with the subjective meanings of places for people. Humanistic geography is in large part a response to perceived inadequacies in the traditional geographical approach to understanding the cultural landscape. That approach, with its goal of objective scientific detachment, fails to grasp the fundamental matter of what it is to exist in or experience the landscape. In their attempts to understand the human subjective experience of landscape, humanistic geographers, understandably, have been heavily influenced by existential philosophy and phenomenological methodology (Tuan, 1971a).

As Cosgrove (1984) observed: 'In geographical usage landscape is an imprecise and ambiguous concept' (p. 13). One ambiguity is evident in the paradox that while landscape was initially employed by geographers to refer to an objectively comprehensible entity, it was subsequently used to identify something which has primarily subjective meaning. Part of the explanation for this can be found in the etymology of landscape. According to *The Oxford English dictionary* and *The Oxford dictionary of English etymology*, the word has antecedents in terms such as the Old English (pre-twelfth century) *landscipe*, which meant region or tract. Of course, in common parlance landscape no longer has this meaning and Sauer, for example, adopted the term as the English equivalent of the *Landschaft* of German geographers. The common contemporary English usage derives from a Dutch term referring to a painting of inland natural scenery. The first English use in this sense - *landskip* - was noted in the sixteenth century. In the seventeenth century, Milton wrote of *lantskip*, referring to a view of the scenery itself rather than to a painting of scenery.

The current use of landscape by humanistic geographers clearly derives from the sense of the word introduced by Milton, although the earlier usage by Sauer and others set an important precedent by legitimating the geographical study of landscape, whatever landscape might be. But, as Cosgrove (1984) ably demonstrated, the painterly or scenic sense of landscape fails to comprehend adequately the subjective experience of landscape because it is the view of a detached outsider, devoid of the perspective of what Relph (1976) referred to as the 'existential insider'. Relph described existential insideness as that form of insideness 'in which a place is experienced without deliberate and selfconscious reflection yet is full with significances. It is the insideness that most people experience when they are at home and in their own town or region, when they know the place and its people and are known and accepted there' (p. 55). While it would seem that the ultimate goal of humanistic geography would be to fathom the experience of the existential insider, the landscape idea implies an outsider's point of view.

Cosgrove showed that the modern concept of landscape developed contemporaneously with the evolution from feudal to capitalist modes of land tenure. As the intimate tie between land and its users was severed with the development of capitalism, the idea of landscape arose. In other words, it became possible to distance oneself from the land so that it could be viewed as landscape. As Shepard (1967) put it: 'Man withdrew from the picture and turned to look at it' (p. 124). The concept of landscape thus has ideological connections with capitalist attitudes towards land. Land has come to be just another factor of production, a form of capital, which has no special significance for or ties to its owners or users. At the same time, landscape can be appropriated by anyone with the requisite sensitivity – 'the right cultural baggage' (Shepard, 1967, p. 132). Both the capitalist mode of land tenure and the idea of landscape imply a degree of control or power on the part of persons who have no specific connections to a place. Planning or development based on such an outsider's view may involve the imposition of alien values on a disempowered community. Reflecting this problem, many of the significant developments in procedural planning theory over the past few decades have been a response to the tensions between the values of insiders and outsiders.

Australian Aboriginal culture presents a particularly interesting example of what I will call, for convenience, the 'premodern' attitude to landscape. The close connection of the Aborigine and the land permeates Aboriginal artworks, including works using primitive materials such as ochres on bark and contemporary paintings using materials such as synthetic paints and canvas. Aboriginal painting almost always relates stories about the land, particularly stories about the creation of the Australian landscape by the primordial ancestors during the 'Dreamtime' (Caruana, 1989). The ancestors, in creating the landscape and the people, animals and plants that inhabit it, traveled along Dreaming-tracks which are often the subjects of Aboriginal paintings. Michael Tjakamarra Nelson's *Possum, wallaby and cockatoo dreaming* (Plate 1) shows the intersection of four such tracks. The possum Dreaming-track extends horizontally across the top of the painting, while the wallaby and cockatoo tracks are the diagonal elements which begin in the lower left and right corners, respectively. The fourth track, indicated by a sinuous line with perpendicular pairs of short lines, is that of the bush banana. Also shown are other sacred elements of the landscape created by the ancestors, sometimes by transforming themselves or parts of their bodies, such as the hills or waterholes indicated by circles of dots.

Much of Aboriginal ritual is designed to maintain the landscape by recreating the actions of the ancestors. Thus the Dreaming-tracks are traveled and the sacred sites are visited periodically. The Dreaming-tracks are also known as 'songlines' because the land was sung into existence by the ancestors and the Aborigines continue to

**Plate 1**  Michael Tjakamarra Nelson, *Possum, wallaby and cockatoo dreaming*

sing the songs of the ancestors while following the Dreaming-tracks: 'In theory, at least, the whole of Australia could be read as a musical score. There was hardly a rock or a creek in the country that could not or had not been sung. One should perhaps visualize the Song-lines as a spaghetti of Iliads and Odysseys, writhing this way and that, in which every "episode" was readable in terms of geology' (Chatwin, 1987, p. 16). This intimate interrelationship of man and landscape is reflected in Aboriginal landscape painting, which does not display scenes or views, but rather flat, abstract, two-dimensional diagrams of sacred places and the events that occurred at those places during the Dreamtime. The modern view of land-scape in painting typically involves the use of perspective to simulate three dimensions and an attempt to portray realistically what is seen from a particular spot in the landscape. Reflecting the importance of automobile travel, Christine Simons' *Emus, Tower Hill* (Plate 2) is framed by a car window. In Simons' painting, the emus are painted realistically as they might typically be encountered in the car park of a nature reserve, while the possum, wallaby, cockatoo and bush banana of Tjakamarra Nelson's painting are

**Plate 2**   Christine Simons, *Emus, Tower Hill*

symbolized by the Dreaming-tracks of the ancestors who created them. The designs in paintings such as Tjakamarra Nelson's reflect those which have been painted for ritual purposes for millenia on bark, sand or the human body. It is only recently that Aboriginal painters have begun to use long-lasting materials, such as canvas, which are geared toward making their paintings marketable. Interestingly, though, painting is still done with the canvas lying flat on the ground, as if the medium were sand.

The antipode of the 'premodern' Aborigine is the modern tourist, with his stereotypical view from the car window. MacCannell (1976) argued that modernity and tourism are 'intimately linked' (p. 3). Modernization is defined by MacCannell as a process that 'separates . . . things from the people and places that made them, breaks up the solidarity of the groups in which they originally figured as cultural elements, and brings the people liberated from traditional attachments into the modern world where, as tourists, they may attempt to discover or reconstruct a cultural heritage or social identity' (p. 13). Instead of the sacred hills and waterholes of the Aborigine, the tourist visits 'attractions' that have symbolic importance

**Plate 3**   Edward Heffernan, *Tourists*

analogous to that of the ritual site. Sightseeing is a 'ceremonial ratification of authentic attractions as objects of ultimate value' (p. 14). By visiting various sights, the tourist can attempt to transform a highly differentiated world into a unified system: 'It is the middle class that systematically scavenges the earth for new experiences to be woven into a collective, touristic version of other peoples and other places. This ability of the international middle class to coordinate the differentiations of the world into a single ideology is intimately linked to its capacity to subordinate other peoples to its values, industry and future designs' (p. 13). The ability of modern tourists to create the landscape in their own images is caricatured rather neatly by Edward Heffernan in his *Tourists* (Plate 3).

While it might be tempting to study landscape aesthetics from the touristic point of view, such an approach would be unduly narrow, neglecting the arguably more important and probably quite different viewpoint of the existential insider. In spite of Cosgrove's warning against the naive use of the concept of landscape, a geographer has quite recently written a book that looked at landscape aesthetics from the viewpoint of the tourist (Jakle, 1987). That book not only failed to take into account the humanistic geographers' concern with the experience of existential insiders, but also disregarded the ideological issues raised by Cosgrove. But such problems are perhaps inherent in the concept of landscape:

Landscape, for all its appeal, cannot mediate the experience of the active insider and the passive outsider ... Geographers who proclaim a human landscape concept need to recognize this as a point of departure, not a problem to be overcome, but a contradiction to be explored in its various contexts. (Cosgrove, 1984, p. 270)

This suggests that anyone proposing to explore the aesthetics of landscape is setting out upon rather hazardous terrain. It does not imply that such an endeavor should not be undertaken, only that the ambiguity of landscape must be kept in mind.

## Landscape, Environment and Place

It might be thought that another term would serve better than landscape. The most likely candidate would be *environment*, as that word is quite commonly used in works on aesthetics by non-geographers to mean more or less what geographers intend by landscape. Some geographers, such as Porteous (1982a, 1982b) even seem to prefer environment. On the other hand, Appleton (1980) defended *his* use of landscape by noting that: '"Landscape" is not synonymous with "environment"; it is "the environment perceived", especially visually perceived' (p. 14). This does not, of course, avoid the bias of the outsider inherent in the landscape idea, and consequently it leads to those problems with landscape discussed above. Thus the philosopher Carlson (1979) objected to the use of landscape, arguing that this 'requires the reduction of the environment to a scene or view' (p. 271). Following Sparshott (1972), Carlson argued that environment is a preferable term because 'to consider something environmentally is primarily to consider it in regard to the relation of "self to setting", rather than "subject to object" or "traveler to scene"' (p. 271).

Appleton's argument reflects not only the bias of the outsider, but also the visual nature of that bias. Cosgrove (1984) has reviewed the connection between the landscape idea and a visual bias in geography, while Porteous (1982b) has noted the need to expand the landscape idea to include the auditory, olfactory and tactile-kinaesthetic aspects of the environmental experience. Sparshott (1972) argued that even proprioceptive senses - such as the muscular sensation while climbing steps - are relevant. Dewey, in his *Art as experience* (1934), had earlier emphasized the fact that experience is not only visual, but also involves smell, taste, touch and so forth. Aesthetic experience is always the experience of objects, with their various characteristics fused together. Porteous and other researchers have done some pioneering work on the appreciation of landscape with senses other than vision, particularly smell and hearing (see *e.g.* Southworth, 1969; Schafer, 1977, 1985; Porteous, 1985; and Porteous and Mastin, 1985). This work on *smellscape* and *soundscape* is notable for its recognition of the insider/outsider dichotomy, thereby avoiding the problems that attend the naive use of the landscape idea.

While Appleton is not correct in focusing solely on the visual nature of landscape, he is undoubtedly correct in emphasizing perception. Thus Maciá's (1979) formulation is more apt: 'The environment is not landscape until people perceive it' (p. 279). Although I shall not be defining aesthetics until the next chapter, it seems safe to assume that aesthetics involves perception and that, to the extent that landscape implies perception, it is a more suitable word for our purposes than environment. Environment is too broad, as it includes things that are not perceived or not necessarily perceived. It should also be apparent that environment shares an objective, scientific connotation with the early geographical usage of landscape. In this sense, it does not seem to be an especially appropriate label for an area of study which is at least partly subjective (*cf.* Cosgrove, 1989), although it is not surprising that behavioral scientists prefer *environmental aesthetics* to *landscape aesthetics*. Finally, while it might be argued that environment is a better term than landscape because it comprises both the urban and the rural scene, it should be noted that the geographical concept of landscape is equally general and subsumes both the natural and the cultural (Sauer, 1963). Thus *townscape, streetscape* and similar terms refer to types of landscapes.

The only other conceivable replacement for landscape would be *place*, because the meaning of place is at least partly defined by the values of insiders (Relph, 1976). It does, however, seem quite odd to speak of the aesthetics of place. This is because – as is the case with environment – place does not necessarily involve perception. According to Relph:

Whether place is understood and experienced as landscape in the direct and obvious sense that visual features provide tangible evidence of some concentration of human activities, or in a more subtle sense as reflecting human values and intentions, appearance is an important feature of all places. But it is hardly possible to understand all place experiences as landscape experiences. (p. 31)

Thus it is reasonable to conclude that landscape is the most appropriate label for our object of study.

### Landscape as Art, Artifact and Nature

A major obstacle in the way of development of a theory of landscape aesthetics is the fact that philosophers have given very little attention to landscape as an aesthetic object. One reason for this is that landscape is not necessarily a form of art, yet contemporary philosophers have displayed an unfortunate tendency to identify aesthetics with the philosophy of art. The titles of two recent treatises reflect this bias: Stolnitz' *Aesthetics and the philosophy of art criticism* (1960) and Sheppard's *Aesthetics: an introduction to the philosophy of art* (1987). Despite their emphasis on art, even these two philosophers were forced to admit that aesthetics cannot be reduced to the philosophy of art or art criticism. Stolnitz observed: 'It is obvious that we apprehend aesthetically not only works of art but also objects in nature' (p. 23). Sheppard went even further by noting that we also appreciate aesthetically artifacts, or man made objects not designed to be works of art. Urmson (1957) summed up the matter when he concluded his attempt to define aesthetics with the observation that: 'whatever the criteria of the aesthetic may be they cannot be found by trying to delimit a special class of objects' (pp. 76–7).

As a consequence of their emphasis on art, landscape has been neglected in philosophers' writings on aesthetics. Landscape is rarely, if ever, just a work of art. Even the most contrived garden is to some extent composed of natural phenomena beyond the control of the designer, and the wilderness landscape consists entirely of natural elements. Furthermore, the everyday landscape is typically a combination of art, artifact and nature, and the relationships among those three categories are complex. One could attempt to force narrow definitions on the three terms by noting that objects of art and artifacts are man-made, while natural objects are not, and that objects of art are intended primarily to be experienced aesthetically, while artifacts have essentially utilitarian functions. But the three categories are not mutually exclusive.

Nature, in particular, has many meanings, one of which includes virtually everything (Tuan, 1971b). In this sense of the word, man and his creations are a part of nature and artworks and artifacts are natural. But, as Tuan remarked, 'the most popular employ of the word "nature" in modern times is as a "catch-all" term for everything that is not regarded as man-made' (p. 4). Even if one adopts the popular usage, it is not always obvious – particularly in the landscape – what is natural rather than man-made. Rural scenes are popularly labeled natural when a small amount of reflection on the matter would quickly reveal that they are to a large extent the result of man's activities (Dubos, 1976). Other landscape elements may resist categorization by reflective observers. Wohlwill (1983) gave the example of artificial lakes: 'If we leave aside ... those created by dams, or perhaps just the portions of those lakes in which the dam or similar artifacts are visible, their "artificial" origin ceases to be discriminable by the average individual' (p. 8).

Like nature, art is a particularly vague concept. Sometimes it is defined so broadly as to seem to include all human activities. At other times it is used in the much narrower sense of *fine* art. In terms of objects, the broad definition encompasses all artifacts, while the narrower definition includes only those objects specifically meant to be appreciated aesthetically. The distinction between the artifact and the work of fine art is not always clear, as some utilitarian objects that would typically be considered artifacts are designed so artfully that they do not fit neatly into one category or the other.

A further blurring of the distinction between art, artifact and nature occurs in the case of art objects that were initially either artifacts or elements of nature. For example, primitive artifacts are often displayed today as works of fine art even though they were not originally created or perceived as such. Modern artifacts have been accorded the status of artworks in the form of Duchamp's 'ready-mades', such as his familiar *Bottlerack*. Moreover, an *objet trouvé* may also be a natural object such as driftwood. Thus works of art may be physically indistinguishable from artifacts or natural objects. This led Margolis (1977) to conclude that 'works of art are *embodied* in physical objects, not identical with them' (p. 48). In Danto's (1964) words: 'To see something as art requires something the eye cannot decry - an atmosphere of artistic theory, a knowledge of the history of art: an artworld' (p. 580). More generally, one might assert that the aesthetic status of an object - whether of nature or of art - is dependent upon the cultural context in which it is experienced.

That assertion has an important corollary that involves another complication of the art/nature dichotomy. This is the claim that aesthetic appreciation of nature is conditioned by art. Apollinaire (1949) wrote: 'Without poets, without artists ... the order which we find in nature, and which is only an effect of art, would at once vanish' (pp. 14-15). Langer (1953) argued that 'natural objects become expressive only to the artistic imagination, which discovers their forms' (pp. 395-6). Noting that both travel and landscape painting simultaneously came into their own in the seventeenth century, Shepard (1967) observed that 'the history of scenery is the history of painting and tourism' (p. 119). Tunnard (1978) noted the relationship between art and landscape perception, particularly the 'close

**Plate 4**   J.H. Carse, *Wentworth Falls, Blue Mountains, New South Wales*

connections between our attitudes to what we see in the landscape and the arts of painting and literature, including poetry' (p. 36). Gombrich (1966) claimed that even the realistic painter can paint only what he sees in the landscape; in other words, what the painter brings to the landscape is just as important as what is there before he arrives.

A particularly salient example of the relationship between art and landscape perception is the major role played by painting and poetry in the development of modern attitudes toward mountain scenery. Shepard (1967) noted the importance of seventeenth century landscape painting in setting the stage for the appreciation of the Alpine landscape which developed in the eighteenth century. During this same period, poets began to describe mountains with terms of praise rather than disparagement (Nicolson, 1962). Coupled with an increasing ease of travel across the Alps, these insights on the part of painters and poets contributed to a complete reversal of attitudes to mountains on the part of the general public: instead of invoking fear or disgust, the Alpine landscape came to be the apotheosis of sublimity (Tuan, 1974). The sublime mountain landscape became a particularly popular genre of landscape painting. Innumerable paintings such as J.H. Carse's *Wentworth Falls, Blue Mountains, New South Wales* (Plate 4) or Eugene von Guérard's *Milford Sound, New*

**Plate 5**   Eugene von Guérard, *Milford Sound, New Zealand*

*Zealand* (Plate 5) both reflect and influence the appreciation of the sublime landscape.

An example from the nineteenth century is Wordsworth's influence on perception of the Lake District in England: 'Wordsworth made the Lake District, already a tourist resort, into what we would call today an object of cultural tourism. He and his sister Dorothy created a landscape of the mind, as those who themselves sought out the scenes of his poetry soon discovered. Like painters, poets infuse their landscapes with values which transform the actual picture seen' (Tunnard, 1978, p. 45). A more recent example of the influence of art on cultural attitudes is the effect of Monet's paintings on the perception of water lilies. According to Bachelard (1970): 'depuis que Claude Monet a regardé les nymphéas, les nymphéas de l'Ile-de-France sont plus beaux, plus grands. Ils flottent sur nos rivières avec plus de feuilles, plus tranquillement' (p. 13). Certainly this is true not only for the water lilies of the Ile-de-France but also for water lilies around the world.

It should be noted that those who propose that aesthetics has a biological basis sometimes make a claim that is quite the opposite of the argument of Apollinaire and the others cited above. The biological contingent argues that the appreciation of art is conditioned by the appreciation of nature. For instance, Humphrey (1980) suggested that planners and architects should: 'Go out to nature and learn from experience what natural structures men find beautiful, because it is among such structures that men's aesthetic sensitivity evolved' (p. 73). Perhaps Humphrey *et al.* and Apollinaire *et al.* were each partly correct and the aesthetics of nature and art are interrelated in a manner more complex than either camp realizes.

In any case, the interconnections of art, artifact and nature suggest that the philosophers' extreme emphasis upon artworks, at the expense of other aesthetic objects, is indefensible. Stolnitz (1960) seemed to be attempting to defend that emphasis with his observation that 'on the whole, nature is deficient in psychological and symbolic interest, compared to art' (p. 51), but that statement seems quite contrary to fact. Indeed, Stolnitz ultimately concluded there is no reason to say that art is aesthetically more valuable than nature.

There are a few contemporary philosophers who have stressed the need to go beyond art in aesthetics. Both Hepburn (1968) and Rose (1976) have expressed the need to extend philosophical aesthetics to embrace nature. Hepburn noted that philosophers' lack of attention to nature is due in part to the indeterminate boundaries or 'unframed' quality of nature. In contrast, works of art are discrete and easy to define (*cf.* Unwin, 1975). Santayana, in his *The sense of beauty* (1961), had earlier commented on the indeterminate form of landscape. For Santayana, landscape referred to natural scenery. He observed that: 'A landscape to be seen has to be composed . . . In fact, psychologically speaking, there is no such thing as a landscape; what we call such is an infinity of different scraps and glimpses given in succession' (p. 99). Thus Santayana characterized the development of the ability to appreciate wilderness landscapes the 'mastery of the formless' (p. 101).

Santayana's observations on the indeterminacy of the natural landscape led Carlson (1979) to the realization that, unlike the discrete, self-contained object of art, 'natural objects possess what we might call an organic unity with their environment of creation: such objects are a part of and have developed out of the elements of their environments by means of forces at work within those environments. Thus the environments of creation are aesthetically relevant to natural objects' (p. 269). Carlson's observation applies equally well to the humanized landscape, which is just as unframed or indeterminate as nature or the natural landscape. This is a very important insight to which I shall return later in this book.

Rose (1976) noted that philosophers were not always so neglectful of nature as they have been in recent decades, citing Aristotle, Augustine and Kant, among others. Kant, in particular, devotes a considerable amount of discussion to the aesthetics of natural objects in his major work on aesthetics, the *Critique of judgment* (1911), originally published in 1790. In his earlier, 'pre-critical' work on aesthetics, *Observations on the feeling of the beautiful and sublime* (1960), Kant attempted to distinguish between the beautiful and sublime as aesthetic categories of human characteristics, but he did not consider any other aesthetic objects. Other contributors to the eighteenth century debate on the beautiful and the sublime – notably, Burke (1958) – applied those categories to natural objects as well.

Contemporary philosophers have given even less attention to landscape than to nature. Langer, for example, in her *Feeling and form* (1953), referred briefly to the problem of landscape at the beginning of the book, but then proceeded to discuss in detail only objects of fine art: painting, sculpture, architecture, music, dance, poetry, prose, drama and film. She devoted only a few paragraphs to the aesthetics of nature, maintaining, as I have mentioned, that the appreciation of nature is conditioned by art. In contrast to Langer, Santayana was one of the few philosophers writing in the past century – he published *The sense of beauty* (1961) in 1896 – who considered the problem of landscape in any detail. I have already mentioned his main insight on the indeterminacy of the form of the natural landscape. He also noted that 'we are usually in a state of aesthetic unconsciousness' (p. 101) with respect to the humanized landscape. By this he means that our attitudes tend to be utilitarian or instrumental. But, as I shall argue in Chapter 2, it is a mistake to attempt to divorce the aesthetic and the utilitarian. An aesthetics of landscape *must* address the practical values that necessarily color the appreciation of the landscape.

By far the most important twentieth century work in terms of its significance for the aesthetics of landscape is Dewey's *Art as experience* (1934). Dewey's book has been quite significant for aesthetics, generally, and Beardsley (1966) described it as, 'by widespread agreement, the most valuable work on aesthetics written in English (and perhaps in any language) so far in our century' (p. 232). Although Dewey's work did not address landscape as such in any detail, his assertion that art is implicit in all everyday experience clearly encompasses the aesthetics of the ordinary landscape. More recently, the philosopher Berleant (1982, 1984, 1985) has elaborated upon Dewey's ideas on the relationship between art and experience in a philosophy of aesthetics which deals explicitly with landscape. Berleant proposed a 'participatory' model of aesthetics which states that landscape as an aesthetic object is neither purely subjective nor purely objective, but experiential: it involves the interaction of subject and object. The ideas of Dewey and Berleant will be discussed in some detail in Chapter 2.

Plate 6   Tom Roberts, *Allegro con brio: Bourke Street, Melbourne*

### Landscape and Architecture

It is useful to look at the relationship between landscape and architecture in some detail because architecture is an aesthetic object very closely related to landscape, and it has received much more attention than landscape on the part of philosophers. Landscape and architecture are similar as they are both aesthetic objects which function as settings for human activity. Given the inclusive geographical sense of landscape, which encompasses both the natural and the man-made, it would seem that the distinction between landscape and architecture is a matter of scope. In this view, the aesthetic objects of architecture are individual buildings and other man-made elements, while the aesthetic object of landscape is defined wholistically to include the entire scene, containing any number of buildings, artifacts and natural objects, including people. The role of people must be emphasized as their presence or absence is often crucial. This point becomes obvious in a comparison of Tom Roberts' *Allegro con brio: Bourke Street, Melbourne* (Plate 6) with Russell Drysdale's *West Wyalong* (Plate 7). While the

**Plate 7**    Russell Drysdale, *West Wyalong*

bustling activity of the former makes it an attractive scene, the absence of people in the latter makes that a scene of stark desolation, unredeemed by the bright Australian light that it shares with Roberts' painting. And the solitary individual in Jeffrey Smart's *Cahill Expressway* (Plate 28; see page 116) is responsible for much of the interest of that scene. The importance of diurnal, seasonal and other periodic changes, as well as meteorological changes, must also be taken into account. W.C. Piguenit's *Low tide* (Plate 8) demonstrates the relevance of both tides and meteorology to aesthetic appeal.

Extrapolating upon the distinction between landscape and architecture outlined in the preceding paragraph, one might assume that in the profession of landscape architecture the relevant aesthetic object would involve the expansion of that of architecture to include not just buildings and other man-made objects, but the entire scene: the landscape. Unfortunately, it is often the case that landscape architecture does not involve buildings in the sense of exercising some discipline over the aesthetic objects of architecture. Instead, all too often, landscape architecture takes up where

**Plate 8**   W.C. Piguenit, *Low tide*

architecture leaves off, usually by beautifying (hiding) with vegetation the excrescences of architecture. To borrow Dewey's comment about the relationship between art and civilization, landscape architecture seems to be the beauty parlor of architecture.

The field known as urban design is in large part a response to the myopic concern of architecture - particularly modern architecture - with individual buildings and the inability of landscape architecture to address that problem adequately. Although urban design is concerned with function as well as aesthetics, the development of that field in recent decades is probably due primarily to a growing appreciation of the fact that the aesthetic object of architecture should not be the individual building, but rather the entire streetscape or landscape.

Although many philosophers - including Aristotle, Hume, Burke, Kant, Hegel, Dewey and Langer - have discussed or at least mentioned architecture, Scruton's *The aesthetics of architecture* (1979) is the first thorough and systematic treatment of the subject by a philosopher. Consequently, much of what follows relies on Scruton's work. Scruton noted that one of the distinguishing characteristics of architecture as aesthetic object is that it is localized. This localized feature of architecture means that a building's aesthetic quality is highly dependent upon the nature of its surroundings and that a building in turn has an impact on the aesthetic quality of adjacent buildings and the entire scene. Thus, in Scruton's terms, a good building reflects a well-developed 'sense of place' on the part of the architect, and architecture is in effect 'an art of the ensemble' (p. 11). Although Scruton did not use the term, that ensemble is probably best labeled landscape.

Appreciation of the implications of the localized quality of architecture clearly leads to the conclusion that the aesthetic object of architecture should be the landscape rather than the individual building. Even though architects are concerned with the design of specific elements of the landscape – usually buildings – their primary aesthetic concern should be with the overall picture. The distinction between landscape and architecture as aesthetic objects would be that architecture implies modification by human agency while landscape does not (even though many or most landscapes do reflect the imprint of human activity). The distinction between architecture and landscape as aesthetic objects is a matter of scope, therefore, although not in the sense initially anticipated.

The close relationship between landscape and architecture is also reflected in the other distinctive characteristics of architecture identified by Scruton. These features of architecture include its functional quality, its publicness and its continuity with the decorative arts. The functional nature of architecture means it is inherently both art and artifact, or craft. Architecture is an object that clearly demonstrates the inadequacy of the distinction between art and artifact because architecture involves a 'synthesis' of aesthetics and function that makes it impossible to separate one from the other. This is the case because 'The functional qualities of a building are of its essence and qualify every task to which the architect addresses himself' (p. 6).

Like architecture, landscape is both aesthetic and functional, and may or may not contain a synthesis of fine art and utilitarian artifact. For example, the wilderness landscape contains neither art nor artifact. In spite of this, wilderness is functional from a human point of view as it affords, to a greater or lesser extent, the means for human survival. In other words the wilderness landscape has both aesthetic and utilitarian qualities. If there is a biological basis for aesthetics, it seems possible that the aesthetics of landscape may be in part based on the degree to which the landscape appears to promote survival. Thus the functional and the aesthetic in the landscape may be intertwined in ways not limited to the synthesis of art and artifact.

The interrelationship of the functional and the aesthetic in architecture is related to the continuity of architecture with the decorative arts. This continuity is shown, for example, in the use of architectural details in furniture design: 'we are never surprised to find a Doric column supporting a wine table, an egg and dart moulding on a wardrobe, a Gothic hat-stand, a Bauhaus corner-cupboard, or a tea-caddy obedient to the law of the Golden Section' (p. 17). Architecture lacks the 'autonomy' of other arts due to the fact that the vernacular arts of architecture and design meld imperceptibly with the fine art of architecture. Because architecture is so bound up with everyday existence, it reflects as much practical exigency as it does refined aesthetic sensibility. As Hume (1888) put it: 'The order and convenience of a palace are no less essential to its beauty than its mere figure and appearance' (bk. II, pt. I, § VIII). Buildings display the practical knowledge of the builder as well as the aesthetic aims of the architect. Just as in furniture design, for example, it is true that buildings are designed as much to 'look right' as to conform to some aesthetic theory. This is also true for landscape. Attempts to modify the appearance of the landscape are typically concerned with what 'looks right' rather than with some canon of the fine art of landscape architecture. The appearance of the garden surrounding a suburban house is almost invariably a reflection of the practical knowledge of the gardener rather than the aesthetic theories of the landscape architect.

Scruton's discussion of the continuity of architecture with the decorative arts led him to conclude: 'Architecture is simply one application of that sense of what "fits" which governs every aspect of daily existence. One might say that, in proposing an aesthetics of architecture, the least one must be proposing is an aesthetics of everyday life' (p. 17). This is at least as true for landscape as it is for architecture. Landscape is the setting for everyday life and, consequently, the aesthetics of landscape is an aesthetics of everyday experience.

A final distinction made by Scruton concerned the publicness of architecture. Architecture's public quality implies that it necessarily has political, social or moral implications. Unlike other art forms, architecture forces itself onto the public; it is inescapable and, consequently, whatever meanings or significances it expresses are unavoidable. Scruton observed, for example, that 'A building may stand as the visible symbol of historical continuity, or equally as the enforced announcement of newfangled demands' (p. 15). The modern movement in architecture was particularly negligent in addressing the publicness of architecture as it tended to emphasize the idiosyncratic whims of the individual architect or the peculiar aesthetic

tenets of modernism rather than values meaningful or even potentially meaningful to the public. Landscape is at least as public as
architecture, and the values it displays are as inescapable as those of
works of architecture.

Although *landscape* is a better term for an aesthetic object than
either *environment* or *place*, it is nevertheless an ambiguous
concept. But this ambiguity presents more of an opportunity than a
problem because it highlights some of the formidably messy issues
that ought to be confronted by any theory of landscape aesthetics.
One issue that must be addressed is the differing values of insiders
and outsiders, and its political implications. Also, the visual bias of
*landscape* must be reconciled with the fact that experience involves
all of the senses. These difficulties, coupled with the fact that landscape is a complex mix of art, artifact and nature, help to explain
why philosophers have generally failed to wrestle with landscape as
an aesthetic object.

Landscape shares architecture's functional and public qualities.
While landscape is not necessarily artifactual, and therefore is not
necessarily functional in the same sense as architecture, it nevertheless displays a meshing of the aesthetic and the utilitarian. This
means it would be a mistake to attempt to somehow abstract the
aesthetic elements of landscape without considering their interrelations with its functional qualities. Similarly, the publicness of
landscape means it would be theoretically inadequate to study its
aesthetic quality without reference to the values it symbolizes.

To the extent that landscape is art or artifact, it shares architecture's continuity with the decorative arts; in its design it reflects
answers to practical questions about what fits. The localized quality
of architecture means that to a large extent architectural design is
a matter of deciding what fits in the context of the surrounding
landscape. Thus it is appropriate to refer to landscape as the relevant
aesthetic object in evaluating architecture.

An intertwining of the aesthetic and the practical is inherent in
the concept of landscape. This suggests that theories attempting to
divorce those two realms by defining the aesthetic as somehow
detached from practical, utilitarian or moral concerns are not going
to be able to accommodate landscape as an aesthetic object. As I
argue in the next chapter, landscape requires an aesthetics of engagement rather than an aesthetics of detachment.

# CHAPTER 2
# AESTHETIC EXPERIENCE

Santayana discussed three levels of aesthetic experience in his *The sense of beauty* (1961). These categories provide a useful starting point for a discussion of the nature of aesthetic experience. Following Lang (1987), I shall label the three levels *sensory, formal* and *symbolic*. For the third of these levels, Santayana used the term *expression*, but it is clear that by this he was referring to an object's ability to express symbolic values. One thing the three levels have in common is a focus on the appearances of objects, or the manner in which things manifest themselves to the senses. Of the three types of aesthetic experience, only the third seems to go beyond the aesthetic object itself to a concern with the *meaning* of the object. Nevertheless, symbolic aesthetics is a matter of how meanings *appear* rather than those meanings *per se*. Tuan's (1989) definition of aesthetic experience as 'largely a matter of the pleasure of the senses, varyingly informed by the mind' (p. 234) seems correct.

Sensory aesthetics comprises such experiences as the feel of a cool breeze on a hot day, or the taste of a peach. The appeal of paintings such as Elioth Gruner's *Spring frost* (Plate 9) and Arthur Streeton's *The purple noon's transparent might* (Plate 10) is due at least in part to the sensory experiences they evoke. Admittedly, such experiences may have symbolic content. For example, the taste of a peach or the feel of the bright noonday sun may be associated with the luxurious relaxation one experienced as a child during summer holidays. But it seems that some sensory experiences are enjoyed for their own sake, without regard to any meanings or associations they may arouse. One must, therefore, allow for sensory experiences as a distinct type of aesthetic experience (see Lynch, 1976, pp. 14-21, for a detailed discussion of the sensory aspects of landscapes).

Experiences such as the feel of a breeze or the taste of a peach would not be characterized as aesthetic by philosophers such as Kant (or even Santayana), who maintained a hierarchy of senses,

**Plate 9**   Elioth Gruner, *Spring frost*

with touch, taste and smell ranking well below vision and hearing. This hierarchy reflects the fact that the visual and aural faculties are closely tied to the cognitive parts of the brain, while the other senses have more direct ties to the more primitive parts of the brain that guide behavior on the basis of feelings rather than ideas. There is consequently a more direct connection between sensory impression and behavior in the case of the so-called lower senses. But this in no way negates the fact that experience is a complex amalgam of perceptions supplied by the different senses. It is unrealistic to single out vision and hearing and claim that those are the only two senses capable of aesthetic perception when, as a practical matter, perception engages all of the senses. Therefore, the position adopted here is the egalitarian one of Urmson or Dewey, who both maintained correctly that aesthetic experience involves all of the senses, at least for the normally endowed person.

According to Santayana, sensory aesthetics is concerned with materials rather than form. This is not a particularly helpful distinction, however, since materials can have symbolic import just as forms do. Consider, for instance, the symbolism of wood versus that

**Plate 10**   Arthur Streeton, *The purple noon's transparent might*

of plastic. Perhaps the best definition of sensory aesthetics is a negative one – it is a matter of pleasurable experience that does not rely on formal structures or any meanings or other symbolic values. Sensory aesthetics would seem to be essentially biological in nature since it involves pleasurable experience that is essentially unmediated by any learned associations. Having said that, there is not much more one can say about sensory aesthetics from a philosophical point of view, since the subject does not seem to lead to any interesting philosophical questions.

Santayana's second category of aesthetics was concerned with the formal qualities of objects. Bell and Fry are well-known proponents of formalist theory. Both were concerned to justify non-representational, particularly Post-Impressionist, art. Bell (1913) went so far as to claim that even in representational art the subject matter is irrelevant. Bell's theory is notorious for the circularity with which he explains his concept of 'significant form'. According to Bell, aesthetic experience involves a 'peculiar emotion' produced by objects with 'significant form'. Significant form is defined as that form which produces the aesthetic emotion. Obviously, the concept of significant form, at least as expressed by Bell, has virtually no explanatory power. Moreover, there seems to be considerable difficulty in isolating the so-called formal elements in a work from the work's other characteristics (Sheppard, 1987). And when there are representational elements in a work, they are by no means irrelevant in aesthetic judgment. The fact that a painting is of a person rather than, say, a horse is something that is obviously taken into account in appreciating and judging its aesthetic quality.

A more recent formalist theory was that set forth by Beardsley (1982c). Beardsley specifically tried to avoid the circular logic of Bell's theory, but it is not at all clear that he was successful. He argued that the fundamental formal properties that contribute to aesthetic enjoyment are unity, complexity and intensity. He attempted to justify these 'primary criteria' by stating that their relevance to aesthetic value is obvious. For example, Beardsley asserted that: 'Anyone who understands that aesthetic enjoyment is (among other things) a relishing of highly organized wholes does not need to ask why unity is a positive critical criterion' (p. 45). But this is patently begging the question, and we are not much better off with Beardsley's primary criteria than we were with Bell's significant form.

Formalist theories of one sort or another have been influential in architectural design and landscape evaluation, and I shall be considering their (often implicit) application to the latter in Chapter 7. One of the most prominent formalist theories in the history of architecture is that concerned with proportion, particularly the proportions of the Golden Section rectangle, the sides of which have a ratio of $(1 + \sqrt{5}):2$. The peculiar attraction of the Golden Section rectangle seems to be the fact that removal of a square formed from the shortest side leaves another Golden Section rectangle. The dimensions of the new rectangle are 2 by $\{(1 + \sqrt{5}) - 2\}$, or $(\sqrt{5} - 1)$, and the ratio of $(1 + \sqrt{5}):2$ is equivalent to that of $2:(\sqrt{5} - 1)$. This means that a façade, for example, could be composed as a set of superimposed Golden Section rectangles.

In spite of the fascination of Golden Section geometry, it is very difficult to translate abstract proportions into concrete experience. Scruton pointed out that it is in most cases difficult to determine, without making precise measurements, whether a building is made up of Golden Section rectangles. Also, because buildings are viewed from many points of view, it is not clear how mathematical proportion can guarantee visual harmony (Scruton, 1979). But the main problem with formalist theory such as that based on proportion is that 'it does not really capture the *meaning* which it purports to analyze ... To provide a "system of proportion" is not in itself to say what "proportion" means or why we should value it' (Scruton, 1979, p. 66). This same criticism applies to the other formal concepts such as unity, complexity, symmetry and so forth. Even 'beauty' is subject to this criticism if it is considered to be a formal quality of an object. Furthermore, as Dewey (1934) noted, 'Beauty is at the furthest remove from an analytic term, and hence from a conception that can figure in theory as a means of explanation or classification' (p. 129). These criticisms do not, however, support the conclusion that there is no such thing as formal aesthetics; they merely state that the formal theories mentioned fail to explain aesthetic value.

One problem that formal theory must address is the fact that aesthetic quality is not just a question of the formal or physical features of the landscape. It is also a matter of what we bring to the landscape in terms of cultural and personal attitudes. Dewey's (1934) critique of Fry's formalism applies not only to artists:

Were it possible for an artist to approach a scene with no interests and attitudes, no background of values, drawn from his prior experience, he might, theoretically, see lines and colors exclusively in terms of their relationships as lines and colors. But this is a condition impossible to fulfill. Moreover, in such a case there would be nothing for him to become passionate about. Before an artist can develop his reconstruction of the scene before him in terms of the relations of colors and lines characteristic of his picture, he observes the scene with meanings and values brought to his perception by prior experience. (p. 89)

Artists and other perceivers of landscape in effect ascribe cultural and personal values to the physical attributes of the landscape; it is impossible for them to view the landscape as if those values or meanings did not exist.

If there is in fact such a thing as formal aesthetics, then it must be transcultural and transpersonal - in other words, biological in nature (*cf.* Lang, 1987). Several biological theories are discussed in detail in Chapter 4. The more convincing of these theories suggests that certain types of landscape structures or forms may be preferred because such features were associated with habitats conducive to survival during much of human evolution. Proponents of biological theories of landscape aesthetics argue that humans have innate preferences for certain landscape forms even though those forms may no longer be important for survival.

Formal theories based on cultural or personal (rather than

biological) values are best viewed as symbolic theories. Such formal theories are typically set forth by artists or critics seeking to justify particular aesthetic styles. Bell and Fry's attempts to justify Post-Impressionist art are an excellent example. Formalist theories, such as those based on the Golden Section, are means of establishing or clarifying what are in fact somewhat arbitrary aesthetic standards. These standards can be viewed as systems of symbolism. Architects who design in accordance with Golden Section geometry are thus employing a standard set of symbols - symbols which will, of course, be meaningful only to others familiar with the system. In some cases, such a system of symbols may be comprehensible only to the artist who devises it. Formal aesthetics is, in many instances, a type of symbolic aesthetics.

The concept of aesthetics as symbolism has a particular philosophical importance because it permits a more complete explanation of significant parallel ambiguities in aesthetics and the idea of landscape. The latter ambiguity was discussed in Chapter 1. On the other hand, the concept of landscape, as it has developed historically, tends to imply the point of view of a detached outsider. On the one hand, to appreciate fully the everyday experience of landscape, one needs to refer to the perspective of the existential insider, who is actively immersed in the landscape. Thus, the experience of landscape is either of two opposites: detached or engaged. This same ambiguity manifests itself in aesthetics generally. While one school of aesthetics - of which Kant is the most prominent member - claims that aesthetic experience is a distinct form of experience that is disinterested and detached from practical concerns, another school - represented most notably by Dewey - maintains that aesthetic experience is a particularly intense, engaged or heightened form of everyday experience.

Different individuals and groups will see different meanings in the landscape and other aesthetic objects due to the differing symbolic systems they bring with them to those objects. In particular, the insider will see things differently from the outsider. The insider will see things in terms of practical significances for everyday life, while the outsider will be largely unconcerned with or unaware of that level of symbolism. According to Sparshott (1972), 'to the transient what he sees is mere façade with no inside and no past; to the resident it is the outcome of how it got there and the outside of what goes on inside' (p. 15). It is in this sense that the insider's experience is engaged, and that of the outsider is detached. In a similar manner, the concept of aesthetics as symbolism helps to explain the differences between philosophers such as Kant, who maintain that aesthetics is disinterested, and those such as Dewey, who maintain the opposite. For Kant, aesthetics was not a matter of the practical significance of a thing; for Dewey, aesthetics embraced the practical level of symbolism and, indeed, is an outgrowth of the most fundamental types of interaction between an organism and its environment.

## Aesthetic Experience as Detached

Stolnitz (1961) has traced the origins of the idea of aesthetic disinterestedness and found it is a modern concept dating from eighteenth century British thinkers such as Shaftesbury, Hutcheson and Burke. These writers began to set aesthetics apart as an autonomous area of philosophical study and, at the same time, the aesthetic object came to be seen as an autonomous entity, defined in terms of distinctly aesthetic rather than utilitarian or other values. Stolnitz noted that: 'This has not always been a commonplace. Indeed, throughout most of the history of Western art, this notion would have seemed not so much false as incomprehensible. During these periods, the values of art are iconic or otherwise cognitive, or moral, or social, with nothing left over that art can call its own' (p. 131).

In Plato's philosophy, for example, aesthetics was not autonomous and he saw close ties between the aesthetic and the moral. In Plato's *Republic* (1937), Socrates maintained that artwork, including architecture, should portray goodness and thereby instill virtue in the citizens of his ideal State. Artists who violated this rule were to be penalized by expulsion from the State. Socrates stated:

Let our artists rather be those who are gifted to discern the true nature of the beautiful and the graceful; then will our youth dwell in a land of health, amid fair sights and sounds, and receive the good in everything; and beauty, the effluence of fair works, shall flow into the eye and ear, like a health-giving breeze from a purer region, and insensibly draw the soul from earliest years into likeness and sympathy with the beauty of reason. (p. 665)

For Socrates, there was no question about the connection between the aesthetic and the moral. That which is good is beautiful to perceive. In the *Symposium* (Plato, 1937), Socrates elaborated on this point by drawing a parallel between the love of absolute beauty, or the *form* of beauty, and love of the good. Because only the forms are real, in contemplating absolute beauty one is beholding realities rather than mere images, and thereby 'bringing forth and nourishing true virtue to become the friend of God and be immortal, if mortal man may' (p. 335).

While it is difficult to accept the Platonic concept of forms and, consequently, the idea that the form of beauty, or absolute beauty, is identical with the good, Plato does seem correct in emphasizing the social responsibilities of artists. To extend Plato's argument a bit, those artists, such as architects, who produce public art, would seem to have a particular responsibility to take into account social or moral values. In this case, the censorship recommended by Socrates is certainly analogous to what we would today refer to as design review. Although we may not go so far as to banish offending architects, we might not allow their buildings to be constructed, which in effect might be the same thing.

In contrast to Plato, the eighteenth century philosopher Burke relied on the autonomy of aesthetics and the concept of disinterestedness in his *A philosophical enquiry into the origin of our ideas of the sublime and the beautiful* (1958). For Burke, the love of beauty did not involve desire or lust. He distinguished the passions of 'general society', which are called love and have beauty as their object, from the passions of the 'society of sex', which are mixed with lust. Just as the love of beauty is disinterested, the appreciation of the sublime is possible only when there is not a real concern for self-preservation. In other words, the delight in the sublime depends on experience of the idea of pain and danger, without the existence of any actual threat. Thus, in both the experience of the beautiful and that of the sublime, the subject is in some way detached from the object.

It was, of course, Kant who was the most systematic in his attempt to distinguish aesthetics by severing aesthetic judgment from the other powers of the human mind. Kant, in his critical philosophy, focused on the distinctions between the logical, aesthetic, and moral or practical faculties of the mind. The aesthetic faculty is that of *taste*, the moral faculty is that of *desire*, and the logical or cognitive faculty is that of *knowledge*. Kant (1911) used an architectural example to distinguish between the faculties of taste and knowledge:

To apprehend a regular and appropriate building with one's cognitive faculties . . . is quite a different thing from being conscious of this representation with an accompanying sensation of delight [i.e., with one's aesthetic faculties]. [In the latter case] the representation is referred wholly to the Subject, and what is more to its feeling of life - under the name of the feeling of pleasure or displeasure - and this forms the basis of a quite separate faculty of discriminating and estimating, that contributes nothing to knowledge. (p. 42)

While the faculty of knowledge is concerned with judgments about objective things, the faculty of taste is purely subjective.

This does not mean, however, that aesthetic taste is subject to personal idiosyncrasy. In regard to this point, Kant argued that aesthetic judgments are disinterested, in the sense that they do not reflect one's personal desires. In other words, they have no practical import because they have no significance with respect to human will. Delight in the existence of something is interest, and interest refers to the faculty of desire, or will, not the faculty of taste. The question of whether a thing is beautiful has nothing to do with whether it exists or not:

All one wants to know is whether the mere representation of the object is to my liking, no matter how indifferent I may be to the real existence of the object of this representation . . . Every one must allow that a judgement on the beautiful which is tinged with the slightest interest, is very partial and not a pure judgement of taste. One must not be in the least prepossessed in favour of the real existence of the thing, but must preserve complete indifference in this respect, in order to play the part of judge in matters of taste. (p. 43)

Because the aesthetic faculty, unlike the moral faculty of desire, is not concerned with practical activity and is therefore not influenced by one's individual subjectivity, aesthetic judgments are universal. That is to say that everyone with 'good taste' - a properly functioning faculty of taste - will make the same aesthetic judgments.

Kant's theory of aesthetics is open to some obvious criticisms, not least of which is the fact that aesthetic judgment is clearly not universal and is subject to cultural influences. Aesthetic tastes differ among different cultures as well as within a given culture over time. Gadamer (1975) has criticized Kant's aesthetics for its failure to take into account 'historical reality': 'The pantheon of art is not a timeless presence which offers itself to pure aesthetic consciousness but the assembled achievements of the human mind as it has realized itself historically' (p. 86). This certainly applies equally well to the aesthetic experience of nature and landscape. Furthermore, it should be noted that personal idiosyncrasies clearly have a significant impact on individuals' aesthetic judgments.

An even more fundamental criticism of Kant is directed at his attempt to distinguish the moral and the aesthetic. As Scruton (1979) argued, aesthetics is a matter of what 'fits', or what is appropriate. Consequently, aesthetic taste is a form of practical knowledge; without it 'a man will often remain in partial ignorance of what to do' (p. 240). People quite often rely on aesthetic judgments as guides to action. Common examples would include the selection of clothing, decisions about how to arrange the furniture in one's home, or choices as to where to go on holiday. Any number of additional examples could be added to this list (cf. Forrest, 1988). Aesthetic judgment is not disinterested and, therefore, it is not distinguishable from moral or practical judgment on that basis.

Like Burke, Kant considered the sublime a second fundamental aesthetic category in addition to the beautiful. Kant, however, distinguished two forms of the sublime: the mathematical and the dynamic. The mathematically sublime impresses by its limitlessness, while the dynamically sublime involves something fearful. As in the case of the beautiful, one who appreciates the sublime is disinterested in the existence of the object. For the mathematically sublime, it is not the object itself that is sublime, but rather the experience of that capacity of mind which allows one to transcend the limits of sensible experience. The actual existence of the object is irrelevant for aesthetic experience. With respect to the dynamically sublime, Kant echoed Burke: the experience of the dynamically sublime involves no actual danger: 'One who is in a state of fear can no more play the part of a judge of the sublime of nature than one captivated by inclination and appetite can of the beautiful. He flees from the sight of an object filling him with dread; and it is impossible to take delight in terror that is seriously entertained' (p. 110). To appreciate the dynamically sublime, one must be detached or protected from any actual threat.

Kant's discussion of the aesthetics of nature and fine art sheds some additional light on his conception of the detachment of aesthetic judgment. Kant argued that objects of nature as a class are usually superior to works of art as aesthetic objects since the former can be appreciated immediately, without the application of concepts, because they do not have the intentional quality often apparent in art. To the extent that a work of art reflects an intention to produce a specific object it is mechanical rather than free, and evaluation of it involves the application of concepts rather than pure aesthetic judgment. Fine art, however, is free because it does not have a specific end or intention. For Kant, fine art, like nature, is 'free from the constraint of arbitrary rules' (p. 166). Thus both fine art and nature can be appreciated without regard to any practical intentions.

The separation of the aesthetic and the practical continues to be pervasive today, and to some extent this continuing division helps to explain the philosophers' neglect of landscape noted in Chapter 1. Landscape is such a messy mix of art, nature and artifact, that it is surely an unappealing object of study for a Kantian aesthetician. The Kantian model works much better if one limits one's analysis to discrete works of fine art such as paintings or sculptures. Philosophers do, however, find it difficult to ignore architecture, yet architecture raises many of the same difficulties for Kantian aesthetics as does landscape.

Bullough, Stolnitz and Beardsley are among the twentieth century thinkers who emphasized the detachment of aesthetic experience.

Early in the century, Bullough (1912) coined the term 'psychical distance' to refer essentially to what Kant described as disinterestedness. For Bullough, distance is a metaphorical term describing the 'peculiar' relationship between the perceiving subject and the aesthetic object: 'Its peculiarity lies in that the personal character of the relation has been, so to speak, filtered. It has been cleared of the practical, concrete nature of its appeal, without, however, thereby losing its original constitution' (p. 91). Bullough gave drama as a clear example of an aesthetic object: in drama, the audience is detached from any practical or concrete involvement in the activity on the stage. He also noted it is difficult to appreciate architecture aesthetically, because most people cannot establish the requisite psychical distance; they are too preoccupied with 'its decorative features and its associations' (p. 98). But what are decorative features and associations if not sources of aesthetic value? The problem here is not so much an inability to appreciate architecture aesthetically as it is the inability of the Kantian model of aesthetics to fully appreciate the nature of aesthetic experience.

Stolnitz (1960) followed the Kantian model very closely. He employed the term 'aesthetic attitude' to denote a type of perception that is distinguished from practical perception. He defined the aesthetic attitude as 'disinterested and sympathetic attention to and contemplation of any object of awareness whatever, for its own sake alone' (p. 35). The aesthetic attitude is one that isolates the object of perception or awareness. But, as Scruton (1974) claimed, 'there is no naked eye' (p. 191). Practical considerations necessarily influence aesthetic values. Stolnitz also asserted that aesthetic perception or awareness is 'positive' and, therefore, an aesthetic experience is 'an experience which is good to have in itself' (p. 42). Here again, I disagree with him, because it certainly makes sense to speak of aesthetically distasteful experience.

Beardsley (1982b) admitted that aesthetic objects can be viewed from different points of view, not just the aesthetic. Not surprisingly, he referred to the example of architecture, citing Vitruvius' three conditions for good architecture: commodity, firmness and delight. These correspond to three different points of view: the practical, the engineering and the aesthetic. Beardsley defined the aesthetic point of view as a concern with certain formal qualities, particularly 'the degree of formal unity and/or the intensity of regional quality' (p. 22). These considerations are obviously quite distinct from the concerns of the practical or engineering points of view.

Elsewhere, Beardsley (1982a) emphasized the detached nature of aesthetic experience. For Beardsley, aesthetic experience is characterized by object directedness, felt freedom, active discovery, and wholeness, in addition to detached affect. Beardsley claimed that the first of these is necessary, and also asserted (rather arbitrarily) that some combination of three of the remaining four criteria must supplement the first for an experience to be aesthetic. He observed: 'It is extraordinarily difficult to capture in words the exact ways in which the practical or technological aspect of an object can and cannot enter into the experience of it if that experience is to have this . . . feature of detached affect' (p. 291). Furthermore: 'It is true that in detached affect there is a lack of concern about the instrumental values, but there need not be a lack of awareness of such values – and in the aesthetic experience of architectural works, for example, such an awareness ought to be present' (pp. 291-2). These statements of Beardsley's are particularly interesting as they illustrate the dilemma faced by philosophers who attempt to fit architecture (not to mention landscape) into the Kantian model of aesthetic experience. Aesthetic objects such as architecture and landscape force one to confront the difficulty, if not the impossibility, of severing the aesthetic qualities of an object (whatever they may be) from its other qualities. In fact, this difficulty led Beardsley to make what is patently a self-contradictory statement: aesthetic experience is defined to be detached from practical matters, yet in some cases aesthetic experience ought to take into account such considerations. This dilemma clearly demonstrates the inadequacy of the detached model of aesthetic experience.

Just as Scruton found, in his *The aesthetics of architecture* (1979), that Kant's division between aesthetic judgment and practical reason is untenable and inconsistent with the nature of architecture as an aesthetic object, so I will have to reject Kant's critical philosophy as a basis for the aesthetics of landscape. Scruton observed that there is no such thing as a purely aesthetic experience of a building in the Kantian sense. He notes that 'Aesthetic pleasure is not immediate in the manner of the pleasures of the senses, but is dependent upon, and affected by, processes of thought' (p. 72). I would put this somewhat differently, since I do allow for the possibility of sensory aesthetics. It is more to the point to say that Kant's separation of the aesthetic and the practical and his claim for the subjective universality of aesthetic preferences are untenable, not only for architecture, but also for landscape. Instead, the aesthetic appreciation of architecture and landscape is inextricably bound up with practical significances for specific individuals and cultural groups (*cf.* Carter, 1976, p. 86).

Lowenthal (1962) cited an excellent example of this from an essay by William James. Here James (1958) was writing about the farms of pioneers in North Carolina:

**Plate 11** Eugene von Guérard, *Old Ballarat as it was in the summer of 1853–4*

Because to me the clearings spoke of naught but denudation, I thought that to those whose sturdy arms and obedient axes had made them they could tell no other story. But when *they* looked on the hideous stumps, what they thought of was personal victory . . . The chips, the girdled trees, and the vile split rails spoke of honest sweat, persistent toil, and final reward . . . In short, the clearing, which was to me a mere ugly picture on the retina, was to them a symbol redolent with moral memories and sang a very paean of duty, struggle, and success. (p. 151)

It is clearly inadequate to attribute these differences in perceptions to dysfunction of either James' or the pioneers' faculties of taste. The different perceptions simply reflect the fact that the clearings symbolize different things to different individuals and groups.

Moreover, such varying perceptions can be found in the same individual. A good example of this is found in the views of Eugene von Guérard, who saw both progress and destruction in the transformation of the Australian landscape in the nineteenth century. Von Guérard worked in the Ballarat, Victoria, goldfields when he first arrived in Australia and later established himself as one of Australia's finest colonial era landscape painters (Bonyhady, 1987). His *Old Ballarat as it was in the summer of 1853–4* (Plate 11) shows a valley completely denuded by the gold diggers. On the other hand, the tents – particularly the circus big top to the left – give the scene a somewhat festive, upbeat air. Jan Senbergs' painting,

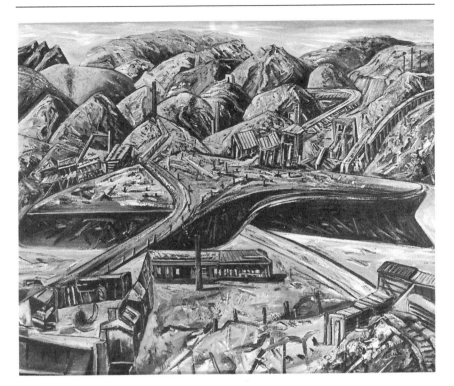

**Plate 12**   Jan Senbergs, *Penghana 1*

*Penghana 1* (Plate 12), displays a similar kind of tension – in this case between the mess the miners have made of this western Tasmanian landscape and the attraction of the purposive human activity the scene represents. Of another of von Guérard's paintings, *Cabbage-tree forest, American Creek, New South Wales* (Plate 13), which illustrates the clearing of the forest by farmers, Bonyhady (1985) observed that: 'the text accompanying the lithograph of the painting, which was published in 1867–8 and which von Guérard almost certainly helped to write, weighed the preservation of the "magnificent" forest against the interests of the farmers. This text concluded that the destruction of the trees, although "unfortunate", was necessary for the progress of settlement' (p. 79).

The point of these illustrations is that the realm of the aesthetic cannot be divorced from that of the practical. Even Kant was ultimately led to draw a connection between the aesthetic and the practical. At the end of his discussion of aesthetic judgment, Kant concluded that the beautiful is the symbol of the moral. This claim seems almost like an afterthought appended to his critique, but Kant

**Plate 13**   Eugene von Guérard, *Cabbage-tree forest, American Creek, New South Wales*

evidently viewed the analogy between the beautiful and the moral as the final explanation of the universal subjectivity of judgments of taste. He wrote:

the beautiful is the symbol of the morally good, and only in this light (a point of view natural to every one, and which every one exacts from others as a duty) does it give us pleasure with an attendant claim to the agreement of everyone else, whereupon the mind becomes conscious of a certain ennoblement and elevation above mere sensibility to pleasure from impressions of sense, and also appraises the worth of others on the score of a like maxim of their judgement. (Kant, 1911, pp. 223-4)

Here, Kant was quite evidently relinquishing at least some of the autonomy of aesthetics, while at the same time capturing the relationship between the aesthetic and the moral or practical realms. If the aesthetic is the symbol of the moral, then this surely has implications for architectural and landscape design. This is one of the reasons why Scruton (1979) emphasized the publicness of architecture. Because the aesthetic is the symbol of the moral and architecture is part of the public realm, the moral values it symbolizes are inescapable.

## Aesthetic Experience as Engaged

Although Dewey's primary statement of his philosophy of aesthetics is in *Art as experience* (1934), he presented an important statement of his basic ideas about art and aesthetics in *Experience and nature* (1929). In the earlier book, Dewey was concerned not to separate art and aesthetics from the practical or the moral:

There are substantially but two alternatives. Either art is a continuation, by means of intelligent selection and arrangement, of natural tendencies of natural events; or art is a peculiar addition to nature springing from something dwelling exclusively within the breast of man, whatever name be given the latter. In the former case, delightfully enhanced perception or esthetic appreciation is of the same nature as enjoyment of any object that is consummatory. It is the outcome of a skilled and intelligent art of dealing with natural things for the sake of intensifying, purifying, prolonging and deepening the satisfactions which they spontaneously afford. (p. 389)

For Dewey, aesthetic experience is consummatory, or inherently enjoyable experience. Any productive or perceptual activity that is meaningful in its own right, not just for instrumental reasons, is art. By this definition, there is no distinction between useful and fine art, as both can be the source of consummatory experiences for both artists and perceivers. The real distinction is between good and bad art, or art that succeeds or fails to be a source of such experiences.

These ideas are developed in more detail in *Art as experience*, where Dewey characterized the separation of art from the rest of experience as an 'ironic perversity' (p. 3) and he set forth the fundamental problem of aesthetic theory as 'that of recovering the continuity of aesthetic experience with normal processes of living' (p. 10). Dewey noted that experience involves interaction with an environment and he argued that aesthetic experience finds its source in the most fundamental types of interaction between organisms and their environments. These essentially biological interactions contain the 'germ' of aesthetic experience.

Dewey recognized, of course, that human experience of the landscape is a much more complex matter than the simple satisfaction of biological needs. For man: 'Space thus becomes something more than a void in which to roam about, dotted here and there with dangerous things and things that satisfy the appetite. It becomes a comprehensive and enclosed scene within which are ordered the multiplicity of doings and undergoings in which man engages' (p. 23). Nevertheless, Dewey observed that people do seem to share certain aesthetic experiences of nature and that this suggests a biological basis for aesthetic experience. The hostility to the idea of merging art and aesthetics with the rest of experience seems to be due to the poor quality of our normal experience, which so often fails to be consummatory. As Dewey put it, 'art is the beauty parlor of civilization' (p. 344) rather than an integral part of everyday life.

Experiences which are complete and unified have aesthetic quality. This aesthetic quality is 'emotional' rather than 'intellectual' or 'practical'. Here Dewey might seem to have been reverting to a Kantian model of sorts; however, he is simply saying that aesthetic experience is self-fulfilling because it involves the direct experience of the qualities of things. Intellectual experience is by contrast indirect, and 'practical' is used here to refer to a concern with means rather than ends. Dewey was quite obviously *not* saying that aesthetic experience is something distinct from what I have been calling practical, everyday experience. Contrary to Kant's model, it is 'Not absence of desire and thought but their thorough incorporation into perceptual experience [that] characterizes aesthetic experience, in its distinction from experiences that are especially "intellectual" and "practical"' (p. 254).

Such 'pragmatic' concepts of art and aesthetics as those expressed by Dewey have been criticized sharply by Langer in her *Feeling and form* (1953). Langer argued that such theories go too far by reducing aesthetics to a matter of animal drives. She saw aesthetics as the philosophy of art: 'The true connoisseurs of art . . . feel at once that to treat great art as a source of experience not essentially different from the experience of everyday life . . . is to miss the very essence of it, the thing that makes art as important as science or even religion, yet sets it apart as an autonomous creative function of a typically human mind' (p. 36). While Langer was correct to emphasize the uniquely human, creative aspects of art, her criticism of pragmatic philosophies of aesthetics was rather severe, at least as it applies to Dewey. As I have noted, Dewey was well aware that aesthetic experience is not solely a matter of biology. He realized that the individual's constitution and environment are cultural as well as biological: 'Experience is a matter of the interaction of organism with its environment, an environment that is human as well as physical, that includes the materials of traditions and institutions as well as local surroundings. The organism brings with it through its own structure, native and acquired, forces that play a part in the interaction' (p. 246). Dewey also noted the importance of the personal contributions of the artist that are reflected in the characteristics of individual works of art; one should add that the individual idiosyncrasies of the perceiver are also significant in aesthetic experience. Thus, in Dewey's thought it is possible to identify three distinct levels of aesthetic experience that could be labeled *biological, cultural* and *personal.* This tripartite scheme will be developed in more detail in the next chapter.

Berleant is one of the few philosophers who have attempted to develop an aesthetics of landscape *per se.* In an essay called 'The viewer in the landscape' (1982), he contrasted the 'panoramic' landscape with the 'participatory' landscape, and notes that these two types can be found in landscape painting as well as environmental design. The panoramic landscape requires an aesthetic of disinterestedness, such as that of Kant, while the participatory landscape requires an aesthetic of engagement, such as that of the phenomenologists. Phenomenology embraces the idea that the objective world is not independent of the perceiving subject, but depends upon the *intentionality* of the subject. The phenomenological view is exemplified in the work of Van den Berg (1955), who wrote: 'The relationship of man and world is so profound, that it is an error to separate them. If we do, then man ceases to be man and the world to be world. The world is no conglomeration of mere objects to be described in the language of physical science. The world is our home, our habitat, the materialization of our subjectivity' (p. 32). This can be contrasted with the positivist emphasis (such as that of physical science) on the objective landscape as it exists independently from individual subjectivity (Seamon, 1982).

While the phenomenologists' emphasis on the subjectivity of experience is an important corrective to the positivist conception of landscape, Berleant (1984, 1985) has more recently characterized phenomenology as being overly subjective. Indeed, Van den Berg's characterization of the world as 'the materialization of our subjectivity' seems extreme. Consequently, in his more recent papers Berleant has posited three models of aesthetic experience: contemplative, active and participatory. The contemplative model refers to the Kantian one, while the active model in these later papers is essentially what was referred to in the earlier paper as participatory. The ideas of Dewey and the phenomenologists are lumped together as examples of the active model. In contrast, the participatory model is neither purely objective (as in the case of the contemplative model) nor purely subjective (as in the active model). Instead, there is a reciprocal relationship between subject and object: 'In this view the environment is understood as a field of forces continuous with the organism, a field in which there is a reciprocal action of organism on environment and environment on organism and in which there is no real demarcation between them' (Berleant, 1984, p. 38; *cf.* Ittelson, 1973; Sell *et al.,* 1984; Zube, 1984).

While Berleant is correct in criticizing the overly subjective approach of some phenomenologists, his characterization of Dewey's

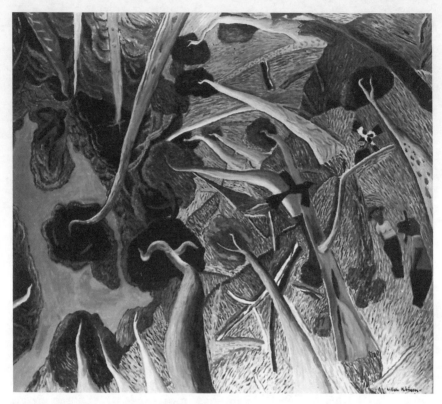

**Plate 14**   William Robinson, *Pee-wee landscape*

ideas seems to involve a misreading of *Art as experience*. Indeed, the primary theme of Dewey's book was that aesthetics is participatory and involves an intimate interrelation of subject and object: 'For the uniquely distinguishing feature of esthetic experience is exactly the fact that no such distinction of self and object exists in it, since it is esthetic in the degree in which organism and environment cooperate to institute an experience in which the two are so fully integrated that each disappears' (Dewey, 1934, p. 249). In effect, both Dewey and Berleant were saying the same thing: aesthetic experience is neither purely objective nor purely subjective, but is a matter of the interaction of subject and object. Carter (1976) has also emphasized this point in his discussion of philosophical issues in landscape aesthetics.

I have suggested that the modern Western approach to landscape painting generally reflects the detached, outsider's mode of landscape experience, while Australian Aboriginal painting illustrates an engaged, insider's mode of experience. Like Aboriginal paintings,

William Robinson's *Pee-wee landscape* (Plate 14) is a participatory work that illustrates the interaction of subject and object. Although the painting displays objective elements of the landscape, its perspective is not that of the detached observer. Indeed, Robinson includes himself, looking up at the Pee-wee (or Magpie Lark) in the upper right of the painting. Although educated in the Western tradition, Robinson is a Queensland farmer who is very much rooted in a landscape. According to Underhill (1987):

during an interview with Robinson . . . he said that he could not imagine why I found his life interesting. He maintained instead that it was all very mundane, he had a wife, six children, taught, lived on a farm, rarely went away or broke his routine and his pictures were about all that because he could only paint things he knew very well like the cows that stepped on him. (p. 21)

While I would not argue that Robinson's view of the Queensland landscape is somehow more *authentic* than that of a casual tourist (whatever such a statement might mean), I would maintain it should somehow take precedence over that of the tourist. Generally, the aesthetic values of existential insiders should have priority, if only because the regular inhabitants of a place must experience their surroundings on a daily basis, while the experience of the tourist or other outsider is only temporary. To use Dewey's terminology, it is arguably more important that a place provide consummatory experiences for its ongoing inhabitants than that it do so for transient visitors. Of course, there is no reason why a landscape could not in some cases accommodate both insider and outsider.

Sonnenfeld's (1966) analysis of this issue led to rather different conclusions. Sonnenfeld contrasted adjustment and adaptation as means for responding to deficiencies in the landscape. Adjustment involves some kind of action taken to correct the deficiency; this could include modifying the landscape or even relocating to a different environment. Adaptation, on the other hand, involves becoming less sensitive to the deficiencies, and therefore does not require any overt actions. Sonnenfeld claimed that not enough attention is given to adaptation as a means for responding to inadequate landscapes. Sonnenfeld further suggests that, while insiders (or 'natives', to use Sonnenfeld's terminology) will have had the opportunity to adapt to or adjust their environment, outsiders (or 'non-natives') will be less placid and may require special efforts to accommodate their tastes. This would seem to suggest that more attention should be given to the tastes of outsiders than to those of insiders.

Sonnenfeld suggested that many of those individuals most concerned with landscape quality are in effect outsiders. This is only partly correct. It is true that planners and designers proposing positive changes in landscapes are often outsiders. On the other hand, insiders will often resist changes imposed from outside which are seen to threaten existing landscape qualities (see Chapter 5). While insiders may be accommodated to the existing landscape, this certainly does not imply they will be indifferent to changes in that landscape. Insiders may have invested the landscape with values not apparent to planners and designers who may therefore propose changes inconsistent with those values. This brings me back to my original conclusion that the values of insiders should have some kind of priority over those of outsiders.

## Subjectivist and Objectivist Theories

Landscape as aesthetic object is properly viewed as the interaction of subject and object: that is, the experience of landscape. There are, however, a number of competing aesthetic theories that would suggest other characterizations of landscape. Some of these theories emphasize the features or qualities of the aesthetic object as if these had some intrinsic aesthetic value without respect to the subjective attitudes which the perceiver brings to the object. Others focus exclusively on the subject. It will be useful to review some of these theories because an understanding of their inadequacies helps to explain why aesthetic value is a matter of the interaction of subject and object and not only the imitative, expressive or formal qualities of the object or the idiosyncrasies of the artist or perceiving subject.

The first object-oriented theory of aesthetics – as well as the first significant theory of aesthetics – was Plato's philosophy of art. Consistent with his philosophy of forms, Plato maintained in the *Republic* (1937) that works of art are merely imitations of reality, because it is only the forms which are real. In fact, works of art are two removes from reality, because they are usually representations of physical examples of the ideal forms, which are themselves only imitations of those forms. To use one of Plato's illustrations, a painting of a bed is an imitation of an actual bed, which itself is an imitation of the ideal form of a bed. Thus works of art are inferior to the physical items imitated, which in turn are inferior to their ideal forms. One implication of Plato's philosophy is that the more precisely a work of art imitates its subject matter, the closer it will be to the ideal form of its subject, and the better it will be.

In his *Poetics* (1968), Aristotle rejected Plato's theory of imitation by observing that art is not just a mirror of life. Although art is a form of imitation (Aristotle observed that it is human nature to learn by imitation), it imitates the essences rather than the particulars of life. Comparing poetry with history, Aristotle claimed that 'poetry is more philosophical and more significant than history, for poetry is more concerned with the universal, and history more with the individual' (p. 17).

Imitation theory, whether that of Plato, Aristotle, or subsequent theorists, suffers from some serious problems. It has been argued, for example, that imitation theory places too much emphasis on what is imitated rather than the work of art itself, and that the work of art consists of much more than an imitation of something (Stolnitz, 1960). Indeed, many works do not seem to imitate anything, but we certainly do not value them any less for that reason. Instead, as Sheppard (1987) pointed out, we seem to value works that display some imaginative effort, or some indication of an effort to go beyond what is merely given. In any case, it is clear that we often do not judge works of art on the basis of how successful they are at imitation, whether of the particulars or the essences of life.

As an explanation of aesthetic value, imitation theory is just as inadequate for landscape as it is for works of art. It is true that some elements of designed landscapes are imitative – one thinks particularly of features of Chinese and Japanese gardens. Speaking of a second century BC Chinese park, Tuan (1974) noted that 'pyramidal islands were constructed in the middle of man-made lakes in imitation of the three legendary Isles of the Blest' (p. 145). But landscape generally is not imitative and it would usually be quite odd to claim that a landscape is aesthetically valuable because it is an effective imitation of something. Indeed, attempts to replicate historical streetscapes (as in Disneyland) may be condemned for their inauthenticity. Furthermore, the natural land- scape is plainly not imitative and, unless one subscribes to some theory such as Plato's philosophy of forms, it makes no sense to judge its aesthetic quality as if it were (Sheppard, 1987).

Although it may be claimed that works of art imitate emotions or states of mind, it seems more appropriate to say that they 'express' emotions. The idea that works of art should express emotions is found in another set of object-oriented theories. In these theories, the degree to which the art object is successful in expressing emotion is the measure of its success. Sheppard identified two variants of expression theory, represented by the ideas of Tolstoy on the one hand, and Croce and Collingwood on the other. Tolstoy (1955) maintained that: '*Art is a human activity consisting in this, that one man consciously, by means of certain external signs, hands on to others feelings he has lived through, and that others are infected by these feelings and also experience them*' (p. 123; emphasis in original). He further claimed that 'not only is infection a sure sign of art, but the degree of infectiousness is also the sole measure of excellence in art' (p. 228). An immediate problem with Tolstoy's criterion is that most works usually considered to be art - including his own masterpieces - are rejected as such by his criterion. As Sheppard noted, by Tolstoy's measure, rock music would undoubtedly score higher than that of Bach. Sheppard also observed that Tolstoy's theory fails to take into account any contemplative or cognitive aspects of art appreciation. Appreciation is simply a passive matter of being infected with the artist's emotion.

For both Croce and Collingwood, art is a form of expression distinct from conceptual expression. Croce (1961) equated expression and intuition, and claimed that art is both expression and intuition. Collingwood (1938) asserted that art is imaginative expression. Both theorists emphasized what goes on in the artist's mind and claim that someone experiencing a work of art recreates in his own mind the artist's intuitive or imaginative experience. Problems with this include the possible incongruencies between the artist's experience and what is reflected in the work of art and also the impossibility of reconciling different interpretations of a work due to the inaccessibility of the artist's thought processes. Even if the artist is available to comment on differing interpretations, his observations may not be reliable, if only because he may not be conscious of exactly what it was that was being expressed (Stolnitz, 1960; Sheppard, 1987). Here again, there is a failure to recognize the contemplative or intellectual aspects of art appreciation.

Expression theory, like imitation theory, is even less applicable to landscape than to art. The salient problem of expression theory with respect to landscape is that it implies an artist. Landscape is only occasionally - and never wholly - the product of an artist. To say that the landscape expresses emotion is far from meaningless, but it is to impute a quality to the landscape that is not intrinsic to it. As Sheppard observed, 'We must study ourselves, not nature, if we want an answer to the question why we find certain natural objects expressive' (p. 58). In contrast, expression theory requires emotion to be embodied in a work of art by its creator. It makes no sense to judge a landscape by the success with which it expresses emotion or infects perceivers with that emotion because expression of emotion is not an intrinsic quality of landscape.

A third set of object-oriented concepts of aesthetics is formalist theory. I have already argued that many formalist theories of aesthetics fail to explain why the formal qualities of objects have aesthetic value and also neglect the attitudes of the perceiving subject. Of course, Bell's formalist theory did refer to a peculiar aesthetic emotion produced by objects with significant form. But the emphasis in formalist theory is clearly on the formal qualities of the object and not on subjective attitudes. Formalist (and objectivist) theory is defensible only when it provides some kind of coherent explanation of the formal sources of aesthetic value. Further, it seems that such theory must be based on human innate propensities to prefer certain types of landscape. To the extent that there is a biological basis for aesthetics, it makes sense to focus on the objective features of landscape; subjective responses to those features will be universal, or at least consistent within biological groups if there is some biological differentiation in aesthetic preferences among groups defined in terms of sex, age or other biological characteristics. Some of the evidence cited in Chapter 4 suggests, for example, there may be such differences in landscape preferences between men and women. In any case, the more universal the subjective response, the more appropriate it becomes to think in terms of formalist theories.

In contrast to theories of imitation, expression and formalism, several theories of aesthetics tend to emphasize the subjective. As I mentioned earlier in this chapter, phenomenological aesthetics is one instance of this. Although phenomenological approaches illustrate the shortcomings of positivist objectivism, they may tend to go too far in reducing everything to the subjectivity of the perceiver. Other examples of subjective theories, such as those of art as make-believe and art as play, focus on the artist's subjective experience. Both of these are related to the more general theme of art for art's sake, or the notion that ordinary life and the life of art are irreconcilable. Oscar Wilde was one of the more notable proponents of this view. For example, in *The decay of lying* (1927), he remarked, 'Art never expresses anything but itself' (p. 615).

Consistent with his theory of art, Dewey (1934) argued that 'art as make believe' fails to realize that art is at best an intensification of, rather than an abstraction from, experience. He also maintained that 'art as play' fails to appreciate the 'work' of art, the fact that the artist's creativity must contend with objective conditions in order that an artwork be produced. Art must be both play and work, both romantic and classic:

What is called 'classic' stands for objective order and relations embodied in a work; what is called 'romantic' stands for the freshness and spontaneity that come from individuality. At different periods and by different artists, one or the other tendency is carried to an extreme. If there is a definite over-balance on one side or the other the work fails; the classic becomes dead, monotonous, and artificial; the romantic, fantastic and eccentric. (p. 282)

Here again, Dewey was emphasizing the importance of both subjective values and objective conditions. In this case, aesthetic value is created as a result of the interaction of the subjective creativity of the artist and the objective context in which the artist works.

Theories of aesthetic experience can be categorized along several different dimensions. One dimension refers to levels of aesthetic experience. Santayana claimed there are three levels - sensory, formal and symbolic. While this division of the subject matter seems to make sense, it must be noted that many formal theories generally seem to be intellectually vacuous and to neglect the importance of subjective attitudes. In some cases, such theories are best viewed as systems of symbolism, meaningful only to individuals and groups with the right cultural backgrounds.

Another dimension of aesthetic theory involves theories which characterize aesthetic experience as detached, on the one hand, and those which characterize it as engaged, on the other. Kant's *Critique of judgment* is the most important statement of the former theory, while Dewey's *Art as experience* is the salient exposition of the latter. I argue that Dewey's theory is correct, at least for the realm of landscape aesthetics, because it is the only one that can properly embrace landscape as an aesthetic object. Among other things, Dewey's theory rejected the artificial separation of the aesthetic and the practical found in Kantian theories. It addresses not only the artistic, but also the artifactual and natural elements of landscape.

Dewey's theory also stressed the importance of the interaction of the subjective and the objective. He argued that theories focusing on only one or the other of those dimensions fail to realize that aesthetic value is the product of the interaction of the two. Theories that focus on the subjective dimension include phenomenological aesthetics, art for art's sake, and art as make-believe or play. Theories emphasizing the objective dimension include the art as imitation, art as expression, and formalist theories. Formalist theory may have a role to play, however, to the extent that there are biological (transpersonal and transcultural) bases for aesthetic value.

Dewey's ideas imply a final dimension of aesthetic theory, one he does not fully develop, but which suggests a particularly fruitful line of inquiry for a theory of landscape aesthetics. Instead of organizing the subject in Santayana's terms of sensory, formal and symbolic aesthetics, it may be more useful to think in terms of biological, cultural and personal levels of aesthetic experience. This tripartite framework for aesthetic experience is discussed in detail in the next chapter, and I shall elaborate on each of the three levels in Chapters 4, 5 and 6 respectively. Among other benefits, such a framework provides the means to go beyond both the biological determinism of Appleton's aesthetics and the cultural determinism of some of Appleton's critics.

# CHAPTER 3
# A PARADIGM FOR LANDSCAPE AESTHETICS

In the previous chapter I noted that there is a tension between biological and cultural explanations of aesthetic experience. On the one hand, philosophers such as Dewey maintain that aesthetic experience is grounded in the most primitive relationships between an organism and its environment. In other words, aesthetics has a biological basis. On the other hand, philosophers such as Langer, who tend to view aesthetics as more or less equivalent to the philosophy of fine art, hold that aesthetic sensitivity is something that distinguishes man from other animals. For instance, Langer (1953) asserted: 'there is no elementary success that indicates the direction in which neurological aesthetics could develop' (p. 38). In this view, aesthetics is strictly a cultural phenomenon. Dewey, however, maintained that aesthetics is not simply a matter of biological drives, but also involves cultural and personal influences.

Appleton, in his *The experience of landscape* (1975a) characterized non-biological manifestations of landscape aesthetics as simply variations in ways of responding to biological needs. Unlike Dewey, he clearly reduced culture to its biological underpinnings. In his discussion of different aesthetic traditions in landscape design, for example, Appleton concluded that: 'All the complexities of Christianity, the Renaissance and Zen Buddhism are based on different interpretations of a common basic relationship between man and his habitat, and it is at this radical, fundamental level that . . . we have been looking for an explanation of the aesthetics of landscape' (p. 228). On the other hand, some of Appleton's critics emphasize the cultural basis of aesthetic experience. There is a tendency to assert that all biological needs are mediated by culture and, therefore, that there is no need to address directly a biological mode of aesthetic experience. Following Langer, these critics assert that there is no evidence in support of a direct biological experience of environment. For example, in his review of Appleton's biologically based theory of landscape aesthetics, Bunkśe (1977) remarked: 'Many others including Shepard, Dubos, and Stea have argued for the continued functioning in modern man of instinctive reactions to the environment inherited from the stone age but their propositions are derived more from common sense than from scientific proof' (p. 150). According to Jeans (1977): 'The survival of primitivist urges in man, like territoriality, is so overlaid by cultural accretions and modifications that it seems uselessly oversimplistic to seek to apply them to human behavior' (p. 346). And Tuan (1976b) wrote: 'In fact, Appleton's book is a tour-de-force of reductionism. The basic idea is simple. People's sensitivity to landscape is fundamentally a biological response to the need for survival in a habitat' (p. 104).

I have been using the terms *biological* and *cultural* to refer implicitly to behavior that is innate and learned, respectively. Much human behavior involves the interaction of biological and cultural influences and it is not at all obvious in most cases where to draw the line between the two. Given the uncertainty about what is biological and what is cultural, it is perhaps not surprising that there is a tendency on the part of some researchers to attempt to simplify things by reducing one to the other by asserting either that all culture is simply a manifestation of biological tendencies or that man's biological nature is subsumed by culture. Both of these attempts at explanation are unsatisfactory because they reduce two qualitatively quite different bases for behavior to one. On the one hand, the biological basis for behavior is transmitted genetically, through sexual reproduction, while the cultural basis for behavior is transmitted socially, through the use of language and other cultural means. This fundamental difference in the developmental origins of innate and learned behavior suggests that explanations based on the reduction of one to the other are inadequate.

Opposition on the part of the cultural determinists to the idea that there are human instincts is probably a reaction to a narrow definition of instinct which involves mechanical or 'closed' patterns of behavior clearly not evident in human behavior. As Midgley (1978) pointed out, human instincts are generally 'open' rather than 'closed' as they do not determine all details of patterns of behavior. In fact, the mechanical definition of instinct is inapplicable to the behavior of many other social animals (Wilson, 1975).

According to Midgley (1978), 'Culture is not an alternative or replacement for instinct, but its outgrowth and supplement' (p. 286). This does not mean that culture is reducible to biology. It simply recognizes the fact that humans remain biological creatures even as they develop highly sophisticated cultures. Even if instincts, or innate behaviors, were always modulated by culture, it would still make sense to speak of a biological basis for behavior in order to attempt to explain behavioral patterns which are due *at least in part* to genetic causes (*cf.* Wilson, 1975, pp. 26–7). Furthermore, if human behavior generally has both biological and cultural components and if one subscribes to Dewey's argument that aesthetic experience is a heightened, more intense form of everyday experience, it is logical to conclude along with Dewey that aesthetic activity has both biological (or instinctual) and cultural (or learned) components just like the rest of human behavior.

While arguments such as Appleton's are rather extreme assertions of a biological basis for aesthetics, there nevertheless seems to be truth in less deterministic statements, such as Dewey's, which allow for both biology and culture and thereby go beyond biological determinism. There also seems to be some truth in Langer's view of aesthetics, although one would have to go beyond her cultural determinism to accommodate Dewey's ideas. If both biology and culture serve as distinct bases for aesthetic behavior, then it is necessary to go beyond both biological and cultural determinism toward a theory which would fully embrace both biological and cultural factors. It is also necessary to consider the role of personal idiosyncrasies and particularly personal creativity, both of which seem to have a certain degree of autonomy from biological and cultural factors. This chapter is therefore primarily concerned with the possibility of building some kind of bridge between the philosophies of Dewey and Langer, a structure that would admit the importance of biological motivation while respecting not only the uniqueness of culture but also the significance of personal creativity and idiosyncrasy.

It must be recognized that the debate between biological and cultural determinism in aesthetics is but a small part of a much larger ongoing debate on the relative roles of 'nature' and 'nurture' in human behavior. The response that followed the publication of Wilson's *Sociobiology: the new synthesis* (1975) shows that this larger debate is very much alive. Wilson's book – particularly his last chapter on human sociobiology – provoked a storm of controversy by proposing what was seen to be a new form of biological determinism. Some of Wilson's statements are tempered by an appreciation of the role of culture, while others reduce culture to biology. As an example of the latter, consider his comment on ethics: 'Scientists and humanists should consider together the possibility that the time has come for ethics to be removed temporarily from the hands of the philosophers and biologicized' (p. 562). Wilson also argued that the development of 'fundamental' theory in sociology 'must await a full, neuronal explanation of the human brain' (p. 575) thus reducing sociology to biology. As Hull (1980) noted: 'Slight as it may be, philosophers and social scientists may gain some consolation from the knowledge that, as the sociobiologists tuck in their napkins in preparation for their feast on philosophy and the social sciences, physicists and chemists are busily gnawing away at the flanks of biology. Reduction in science gives every appearance of a many-headed hydra attempting to consume itself' (p. 78). The point is that just as biology cannot be reduced to physics and chemistry, culture cannot be reduced to biology.

Much of the seductive appeal of human sociobiology for its proponents seems to be that it provides plausible explanations for many aspects of human behavior. Sociobiological explanation tends to assume that human morphology and behavior result from natural selection and, to the extent that one can argue that a specific behavior is biologically adaptive, one has identified a plausible biological basis for behavior. There are serious pitfalls in this kind of reasoning because not all adaptive behavior results from natural selection and there are various possible explanations for each pattern of behavior (Gould, 1980). As Gould observed, human sociobiology is even more speculative than animal sociobiology because: 'We have little direct evidence about the genetics of behavior in humans' (p. 262). Furthermore:

Much of human behavior is clearly adaptive, but the problem for sociobiology is that humans have so far surpassed all other species in developing an alternative, non-genetic system to support and transmit adaptive behavior - cultural evolution. An adaptive behavior does not require genetic input and Darwinian selection for its origin and maintenance in humans; it may arise by trail and error in a few individuals that do not differ genetically from their groupmates, spread by learning and imitation, and stabilize across generations by value, custom and tradition. Moreover, cultural transmission is far more powerful in potential speed and spread than natural selection - for cultural evolution operates in the 'Lamarckian' mode by inheritance through custom, writing and technology of characteristics acquired by human activity in each generation. (p. 264)

Human sociobiology too often fails to appreciate the significance of the qualitative distinction between biological and cultural evolution.

In commenting on sociobiology and the question of biological versus cultural determinism, the anthropologist Silverberg (1980) noted that his discipline has long been concerned with both biology and culture and that therefore the 'new' synthesis proposed by Wilson is actually an 'old' one. Furthermore, he argued that Wilson's sociobiology is not a synthesis at all but a reduction of culture to biology. Rappaport (1986) similarly argued that anthropology involves a synthesis of both the biological and the cultural. While it is possible that anthropology might provide a useful paradigm for aesthetic theory, I am going to suggest instead a paradigm developed by the Russian psychologist Vygotsky.

### Beyond Biological and Cultural Determinism: Vygotsky's Paradigm

One route beyond biological and cultural determinism is suggested by Bachelard in his *The poetics of space* (1969). In that book, Bachelard is concerned with poetic images of 'felicitous space' and, as a basis for the study of such images, he sets forth a rather provocative philosophy. His philosophy emphasizes the creativity manifested in art, but it also embraces, at least implicitly, both the cultural and the biological bases of behavior. Quoting Jung, Bachelard suggests that human mental structure can be used as a model for aesthetic analysis. Using a metaphor, Jung (1928) characterized the problem of describing the mind as follows:

we have . . . to describe and to explain a building the upper story of which was erected in the nineteenth century; the ground floor dates from the sixteenth century, and a careful examination of the masonry discloses the fact that it was reconstructed from a dwelling-tower of the eleventh century. In the cellar we discover Roman foundation walls, and under the cellar a filled-in cave, in the floor of which stone tools are found, and remnants of glacial fauna in the layers below. That would be a sort of picture of our mental structure. We live in the upper story, and are only dimly aware that our lower story is somewhat old-fashioned. As to what lies beneath the superficial crust of the earth we remain quite unconscious. (pp. 118-9; quoted in part by Bachelard, 1969, p. xxxiii)

It should be noted that the foundations are active in the mind and not inert as might be implied by the metaphor.

The idea that human mental structure can serve as a basis for aesthetic analysis has considerable intuitive appeal, as it is obvious that aesthetic experience must be mediated by the mind and, therefore, may be a reflection of the structure of the mind. I have observed elsewhere that Jung's conception of mind provides a basis for integrating biological and cultural bases for behavior (Bourassa, 1988). In particular, Jung's division of the mind into three levels - consciousness, the personal unconscious and the collective unconscious - provides a structure that allows for both biological and cultural influences on behavior. The archetypes, which are contained in the collective unconscious, are 'patterns' of instinctual or biologically based behavior (Jung, 1928, 1959). On the other hand, consciousness and the personal unconscious provide a locus for culturally based influences on behavior. Jung was interested primarily in the collective unconscious and its contents, the archetypes.

Although Jung's ideas are quite helpful in developing an integrated framework for landscape aesthetics, it must be recognized that the problems he addressed were not congruent with the general problem of reconciling biological and cultural explanations of behavior. In a sense, it could be said that his concerns were more specific. On the one hand, he emphasized the biological basis for behavior through his focus on the collective unconscious and the archetypes. On the other, he criticized the negative effects of culture as it is manifested in what he called the *persona*. The persona is, in effect, the individual's socially created identity, an identity that can be in conflict with more fundamental, archetypal foundations for behavior – *i.e.*, the 'primitive psyche' (Jung, 1964, p. 98). As an example, Jung criticized religious dogma as interfering with direct religious experience, such as that of an archetypal god-like imago (Homans, 1979). By focusing on the specific problem of the persona, Jung did not fully address cultural bases for behavior, so as to encompass their more general and positive attributes. This is not to discount the potential relevance of Jung's ideas to various aspects of landscape aesthetics (see *e.g.* Tyng, 1969 and Cooper, 1974).

In contrast to Jung, the Russian psychologist Vygotsky provided a more general account of human mental structure and behavior. Vygotsky's methodological approach to this problem was 'developmental' since he explained the structures of the mind by reference to their origins and processes of development. Jung's approach was also developmental, just not as comprehensive as Vygotsky's. In the following passage, for example, Jung (1964) was explicit about his emphasis on biological evolution:

Just as the human body represents a whole museum of organs, each with a long evolutionary history behind it, so we should expect to find that the mind is organized in a similar way. It can no more be a product without history than is the body in which it exists. By 'history' I do not mean the fact that the mind builds itself up by conscious reference to the past through language and other cultural traditions. I am referring to the biological, prehistoric, and unconscious development of the mind in archaic man, whose psyche was still close to that of the animal. (p. 67)

Vygotsky was a prolific and original psychologist who died in 1934 at the age of 37. Toulmin (1978) has characterized him as 'the Mozart of psychology'. For various reasons, Vygotsky's ideas have not received as much attention as they deserve. For two decades after his death, Vygotsky was officially a 'non-person' in the Soviet Union due to the incompatibility of his ideas with those of Stalin. While Vygotsky tried to accommodate both biological and cultural explanations of behavior, 'Stalin insisted that *all* phenomena were "culturally conditioned," and so amenable to technological transformation by human intervention' (Toulmin, 1978, p. 51). As a result of this, Vygotsky's ideas were never developed in the Soviet Union to the extent they probably should have been. English-speaking researchers have not had much exposure to his ideas because his works have been slow to appear in English and there are still relatively few translations available.

Vygotsky's developmental approach to understanding the human mind and human behavior is particularly insightful because it goes beyond mere description to explanation of the underlying processes. This method stands in sharp contrast to the most commonly employed research models in landscape aesthetics, which yield descriptions rather than explanations (Zube *et al.*, 1982). Vygotsky maintained that, by studying the *processes* of development rather than the *product* of development, it becomes possible to explain, rather than simply describe behavior (Wertsch, 1985). He argued that, in order to comprehend human behavior, it is necessary to understand biological evolution, the historical development of culture and the processes by which individuals develop. Vygotsky's emphasis on a developmental approach to understanding human behavior resulted in a tripartite scheme combining phylogenesis (or biological evolution), sociogenesis (or cultural history) and ontogenesis (or individual development). In *Essays in the history of behavior: ape, primitive, child*, Vygotsky and Luria stated:

Our task [in this volume] was to trace *three basic lines* in the development of behavior – the evolutionary, historical, and ontogenetic lines – and to show that the behavior of acculturated humans is the product *of all three lines* of development, to show that behavior can be understood and explained scientifically only with the help of *three different paths from which the history of human behavior takes place.* (cited by Wertsch, 1985, p. 27)

Much of Vygotsky's research was concerned with explicating the processes of ontogenesis; however, he did address the other lines of development. Vygotsky viewed phylogenesis as Darwinian evolution. Also, according to Wertsch (1985): 'Inherent in Vygotsky's account of organic evolution is the claim that it proceeds up to a point where culture can emerge, and then this evolution ceases. He envisioned virtually no overlap between the two types of genesis' (p. 29). This is not supported by the evidence, however, because evolution continued after human culture emerged. Indeed, it is quite possible that culture influences the path of biological evolution (Butzer, 1977). For example, Livingstone (1980) argued that genetic variations in the ability to metabolize alcohol and digest lactose correspond with long-term cultural variations in the consumption of alcohol and milk, respectively, and probably represent genetic adaptations.

With regard to cultural history, Vygotsky (1981c) focused on the development of psychological tools, or *signs*, which he viewed as the distinguishing features of the human species. In Wertsch's (1985) unfortunately clumsy terminology, Vygotsky's principle of cultural development was that of the 'decontextualization of mediational means', or 'the process whereby the meaning of signs becomes less dependent on the unique spatiotemporal context in which they are used' (p. 33). Scribner (1985) noted that one problem with Vygotsky's account of cultural development is his tendency to view history as a single course of development: 'But for purposes of concrete research, and for theory development in the present, such a view seems inadequate. Societies and cultural groups participate in world history at different tempos and in different ways' (p. 139). But Vygotsky's ideas *are* generally consistent with the observations of philosophers such as Cassirer (1944) and Midgley (1978), who have identified man's highly developed ability to use and interpret symbols as his most significant distinguishing feature. There is, however, a significant difference between the points of view of Cassirer and Midgley. Midgley emphasizes the continuities between man and other animals while Cassirer emphasizes the discontinuities. A good part of the basis for this difference is the fact that, when Cassirer was writing, scientists had not yet succeeded in teaching chimpanzees and gorillas to use sign language. (In this regard, it is interesting to compare Cassirer's discussion of chimpanzee behavior with Midgley's.)

Both biological (Vygotsky uses the word *natural*) and cultural influences work together in ontogenesis. As individuals mature biologically, they are also acculturated. Vygotsky (1981a) notes that the natural line of development in ontogenesis parallels in some ways the processes of phylogenesis, but he is rather vague on this point. As Wertsch (1985) observed, Vygotsky never did explain clearly what is meant by 'natural' in the context of ontogenesis. In contrast, Vygotsky's conception of the cultural line of development in ontogenesis is fairly well developed. This line of development parallels the general historical development of culture; in Wertsch's cumbersome terminology, it is a process of decontextualization of mediational means. Vygotsky (1978) referred to this process as *internalization*. In Vygotsky's (1981a) words: 'We know that the general sequence of the child's cultural development consists of the following: At first other people act on the child. Then he/she emerges or enters into interaction with those around him/her. Finally, he/she

**Table 1**   Processes and products of development as identified by developmental and phenomenological methods

| Processes of development | | Products of development |
|---|---|---|
| Phylogenesis | ————————▶ | *Umwelt* |
| Sociogenesis | ————————▶ | *Mitwelt* |
| Ontogenesis | ————————▶ | *Eigenwelt* |

begins to act on others, and only at the end begins to act on himself/herself' (p. 220). This same general process applies to the development of psychological tools. Signs, which are initially external to the child, are internalized. The ultimate level of development is that of intellectual response (Vygotsky, 1981b) in which the individual uses signs internally to affect his own behavior.

It is interesting to note the parallels between Vygotsky's development paradigm and the independently developed concepts of the existential movement in psychiatry. As May (1958b) observed, the existential movement in psychiatry seeks 'to analyze the structure of human existence' (p. 7). One result of that analysis is the identification of three simultaneous modes of existence, the *Umwelt*, the *Mitwelt* and the *Eigenwelt* (May, 1958a). These three terms were first applied by the Swiss psychiatrist Binswanger, who also founded existential analysis or *Daseinsanalyse* (Ellenberger, 1958). These are essentially the products of the developmental processes identified by Vygotsky (Table 1).

The first of the three modes is the biological world. According to May (1958a):

For animals and human beings the *Umwelt* includes biological needs, drives, instincts - the world one would exist in if, let us hypothesize, one had no self-awareness. It is the world of natural law and natural cycles, of sleep and awakeness, of being born and dying, desire and relief, the world of finiteness and biological determinism, the 'thrown world' to which each of us must in some way adjust. (p. 61)

The second mode of human existence - the *Mitwelt* - is the social or cultural world: 'the world of interrelationships with human beings' (p. 62). The last mode - the *Eigenwelt* - is one's personal world: 'the mode of one's relationship to one's self' (p. 61). Here it is implied that the individual is mature, or, in Vygotsky's (1981a) terms, has developed to the 'stage of intellectual responses' (pp. 172-5). Otherwise, it would be difficult to understand what is meant by 'one's relationship to one's self'. At the stage of intellectual responses, the individual has internalized language and uses it as a tool to influence his own behavior. Behavior is no longer strictly the

**Table 2** Modes of existence and corresponding modes of aesthetic experience

| Modes of existence | | Modes of aesthetic experience |
|---|---|---|
| *Umwelt* | ⟶ | Biological |
| *Mitwelt* | ⟶ | Cultural |
| *Eigenwelt* | ⟶ | Personal |

result of biologically-determined and culturally-conditioned responses.

It is tempting to translate the three modes of existence into three corresponding modes of aesthetic experience (Table 2). As I have already mentioned, Dewey's theory of aesthetics suggests such a tripartite organization of the subject. One can see such a framework presaged even more clearly in the work of the eighteenth century philosopher Hume (1965). Hume is best known for his influential empiricist theory of knowledge, and it is not surprising that his theory of aesthetics reflects an empiricist concern with the phenomenology of human nature. Thus Hume's theory shows remarkable parallels with the tripartite theory I have derived from Vygotsky's developmental psychology and the existentialists' phenomenological account of the nature of human existence. Hume noted that humans seem to have certain tastes in common and concludes: 'It appears then, that, amidst all the variety and caprice of taste, there are certain general principles of approbation or blame, whose influence a careful eye may trace in all operations of the mind' (p. 9). Such universal principles would presumably be innate, or biological, bases for aesthetic tastes. There are, however, two sources of variation in taste: 'The one is the different humours of particular men; the other, the particular manners and opinions of our age and country' (p. 19). These two sources of variation correspond to what I am labeling, respectively, personal and cultural bases for aesthetics. In his *Treatise of human nature* (1888), Hume also suggested a tripartite basis for aesthetics: 'beauty is such an order and construction of parts, as either by the *primary constitution* of our nature, by *custom*, or by *caprice* is fitted to give a pleasure and satisfaction to the soul' (bk. II, pt. I, § VIII).

While it is tempting to translate the three modes of existence into three corresponding modes of aesthetic experience, this leaves unanswered questions about the interrelations of the three modes. Following Vygotsky, we could assert that both biological and cultural factors underlie the personal mode, and that the individual can transcend those constraints through intellectual activity. But this does not explain how biological and cultural factors interrelate in aesthetic experience of landscape. In other words, are there distinct biological and cultural modes of aesthetic experience, or are these two modes inextricably intertwined?

## Evidence of Distinct Biological and Cultural Modes of Experience

While it is certainly not possible to prove there are distinct 'biological' and 'cultural' modes of experience, there is evidence that suggests there may be dual modes of perception. Neurophysiological research has shown that different parts of the brain specialize in innate and learned behaviors and that the visual and other sensory systems have direct connections to each of these different parts. The work of the neurophysiologist MacLean is particularly important (see *e.g.* MacLean, 1973a, 1973c) and will be discussed in some detail. Further evidence from experimental psychology and 'blindsight' research gives some preliminary clues about the nature of the different perceptual modes. In experimental psychology, the work of Zajonc and his colleagues is especially significant (see *e.g.* Zajonc, 1980), as is the research on 'blindsight' by Weiskrantz and others (see *e.g.* Weiskrantz, 1987).

According to MacLean, the human brain is divided into three parts that he calls reptilian, paleomammalian and neomammalian (Plate 15). Both in terms of structure and function, the reptilian and paleomammalian brains are similar to their counterparts in the brains of more primitive animals (Plate 16). The neomammalian brain (or neocortex) is more distinctly human and is the seat of those capabilities such as language that are found primarily in man. In regard to the reptilian brain, MacLean (1973c) noted: 'On the basis of behavioural observations of ethologists, there are indications that the reptilian brain programs stereotyped behaviours according to instructions based on ancestral learning and ancestral memories' (p. 8). The paleomammalian, or limbic, brain: 'acts upon information in terms of feelings, particularly emotional feelings that guide behavior with respect to the two basic life principles of *self-preservation* and *the preservation of the species*' (MacLean, 1962, p. 289; see also MacLean, 1958a, 1958b, 1959).

MacLean's conclusions with respect to the limbic brain are based on the results of an extensive series of experiments conducted by himself and others. These experiments typically involved electrical or chemical stimulation of the brains of animals such as cats, rats and squirrel monkeys. Some of the experiments involved the removal of portions of or introduction of lesions in the animals'

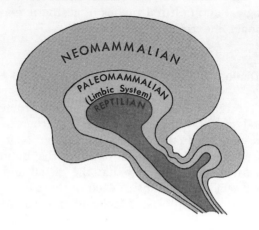

**Plate 15**   Tripartite structure of the human brain

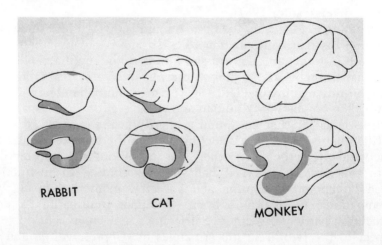

**Plate 16**   Limbic systems of rabbit, cat and monkey

brains. These experiments have revealed that certain regions of the limbic brain are active in self-preservation and preservation of the species, respectively. For example, stimulation of certain parts of the limbic brain results in alimentary activities such as licking and eating or activities related to searching for food and self-defense. Stimulation of other parts results in responses related to the preservation of the species, such as intensified grooming and sexual excitement. In the case of the human brain, the experiences of persons suffering damage to the relevant parts of the limbic brain are comparable to the experimental results with animals. Epileptic patients with damage to the portion of the limbric brain linked with self-preserving activities in animals will, during seizures, experience symptoms related to alimentation or unpleasant emotional feelings related to the struggle for survival (MacLean, 1958b).

Research on brain physiology has also revealed direct connections between the visual and other sensory systems and both the limbic brain and the neocortex (MacLean, 1973b, 1973d; Moore, 1973; Gloor, 1978). For example, using microelectrodes to study the limbic brains of squirrel monkeys, MacLean (1973b) located nerve cells which respond to ocular illumination. And Weiskrantz (1986) observed that while about 90 percent of optic nerve fibers are connected with the visual cortex, 'there are at least 6 other branches that end up in the mid-brain and subcortical regions . . . and one of these contains about 100,000 fibres, by no means a trivial pathway – it is larger than the whole of the auditory nerve' (p. 5). These connections help to explain why individuals suffering damage in certain parts of their limbic brains will experience hallucinations and other visual distortions.

The neurophysiological research findings discussed in the preceding paragraphs suggest that instinctual and emotional responses to landscape *could* occur separately from rational and cognitive responses. In other words, there could be separate innate and learned responses to landscape. Furthermore, since the phylogenetically 'new' and 'old' sections of the brain respond to perceptions in different ways, it is possible that conflicting instinctual and rational responses to landscapes could occur simultaneously. As Greenbie (1973) put it, 'We may assume that each of us lives, not in one environment, but two environments simultaneously' (p. 16). Referring to MacLean's research, Greenbie argued for a distinction between 'limbic' and 'conceptual' space. And as Smith (1977) suggested, perception and response may be 'limbic intensive' in that instinctual behavior may overwhelm rational behavior.

Perhaps the most intriguing body of research that suggests there are dual limbic and neocortical perceptual systems involves the phenomenon of 'blindsight'. Humphrey's (1970, 1972) studies of blindsight in monkeys and Weiskrantz's (1986) case study of human blindsight are particularly noteworthy. Weiskrantz, who coined the term, defined human blindsight as 'visual capacity in a field defect in the absence of acknowledged awareness' (p. 166). Blindsight, in other words, refers to the ability of an individual with impaired vision to react to visual phenomena without any consciousness of those phenomena. The visual impairment in blindsight studies is in the form of damage to the visual cortex, suggesting that the residual visual capacity is a function of lower brain structures.

Humphrey's research focused primarily on the behavior of one monkey, Helen, whose visual cortex had been surgically removed. Although she seemed to be completely blind immediately after the operation, she eventually developed an ability to detect objects in her environment. She remained, however, unable to perceive or comprehend patterns or spatial arrangements – Humphrey (1972) noted she was unable to recognize a carrot or even his face. She could detect visual objects, but had no knowledge of what they were. Extrapolating from his experience with Helen, Humphrey (1970) assumed that subcortical structures play a similar role in animals with normal vision: 'they provide an articulated visual field' (p. 335). In an animal with an intact visual cortex, the detection of objects by subcortical structures serves as a basis for their classification by the visual cortex (something that Helen could not do), thereby 'making possible cognitive visual behavior' (p. 336).

Weiskrantz's research involved primarily one human subject, identified as 'D.B.' The right side of D.B.'s visual cortex was removed surgically in order to excise a tumorous mass of blood vessels. The operation initially resulted in the loss of the left half-field of vision in both eyes. Over the next several years, however, D.B. regained normal vision in the upper left quadrant of each eye. Through an extensive series of studies over a period of ten years, Weiskrantz tested the residual visual ability in D.B.'s field defects. This was accomplished with 'forced choice' tests in which an object was presented to D.B.'s 'blind' field and he was forced to make some choice which would reveal whether he was subconsciously aware of the object.

Although D.B. repeatedly claimed he was unable to see in any normal sense objects presented to his defective field, he was often able to react to those objects. For instance, he could quite effectively point to objects that he could not 'see' as well as detect the presence or absence of an object. He could also discriminate the orientation of bars presented either horizontally or vertically and accomplish a number of other tasks described in detail by Weiskrantz (1986). Weiskrantz designed his experiments to eliminate both the possibility that D.B.'s residual abilities were actually a product of his normal visual field and the possibility that those abilities were simply a degraded form of normal vision. Indeed, Weiskrantz concluded that D.B.'s residual abilities 'are precisely the discriminative capacities that have been demonstrated in monkeys with confirmed destruction of the striate [*i.e.*, visual] cortex, and moreover, as far as one can judge, they are quantitatively of the same order of magnitude' (p. 157). In other words, it is extremely unlikely that D.B.'s residual abilities were a function of his remaining visual cortex. Weiskrantz concluded, therefore, that the dual visual system hypothesis is the best explanation of D.B.'s behavior.

Paillard *et al.* (1983) have reported the case of a patient with tactile abilities analogous to blindsight. The patient suffered from anesthesia in her right side and could injure herself severely without noticing it. The anesthesia was an accidental side effect of an operation to correct an obstruction in a cerebral artery. In spite of the anesthesia, the patient was able to respond to static pressure on her right hand. While blindfolded, she could point with some accuracy with her left hand to the spot touched on her right hand. Furthermore, she only pointed when her hand had been touched, never doing so during a false trial. The authors noted, however, that it was not possible to attribute this conclusively to subcortical processing because the patient may have retained some relevant cortical functions. They also noted that 'we are limited, as yet, by our rudimentary knowledge of the subcortical and cortical processing of somatesthetic afferents, as compared with the steadily increasing understanding of the multichanneling of visual afferents' (p. 551). Nevertheless, Paillard *et al.*'s findings are quite consistent with the hypothesis of dual perceptual systems.

Izard (1984) noted that: 'although emotion and cognition are in large measure *interdependent*, another body of evidence suggests as well that emotion processes and cognitive processes have a significant degree of independence' (p. 23). Much of the body of evidence to which Izard referred has been produced by Zajonc and his colleagues. Writing in 1980, Zajonc observed that contemporary psychology assumed that feeling follows cognition. In other words, affective states were considered to occur only after significant cognitive processing (*cf.* Tomkins, 1981). Zajonc noted that this assumption was rather odd, given the lack of evidence to support it and the fact that one of the early psychologists, Wundt, observed that affective states often precede cognition. Zajonc and others (*e.g.* Moreland and Zajonc, 1977; Wilson, 1979; and Kunst-Wilson and Zajonc, 1980) have conducted a series of ingenious experiments that demonstrate preferences for stimuli may develop even in the absence of any cognitive knowledge of those stimuli. (There is, however, some debate on this issue. See Birnbaum, 1981; Zajonc, 1981, 1984; Lazarus, 1982, 1984.)

For example, Kunst-Wilson and Zajonc (1980) devised an experiment involving the recognition of and affective response to a set of randomly generated, irregular octagons. The experiment relied on previous research demonstrating that repeated exposure to a stimulus increases its attractiveness. This phenomenon is known as the *exposure effect*. Thus repeated exposure to an irregular octagon should increase its attractiveness relative to that of an octagon never before seen. In the exposure phase of the experiment, the octagons were divided into two sets that were shown to two sets of subjects. The duration and illumination of each exposure were reduced to the point at which the subjects could not discern what was being shown. Subsequently, in the test phase of the experiment, each subject was required to compare pairs of slides, one of each pair from the set to which the subject had been exposed and one from the other set. While the subjects could not recognize the octagons to which they had been exposed, they did have a decided preference for those octagons. As the authors concluded: 'Individuals can apparently develop preferences for objects in the absence of conscious recognition and with access to information so scanty that they cannot ascertain whether anything at all was shown' (p. 558).

Previous experiments by Wilson (1979) involved auditory perception of stimuli. In these experiments, subjects listened to a story presented to one ear while sequences of tones were presented to the other ear. In the more successful experiments, the subjects were required to repeat each word after it was spoken and simultaneously proofread a written version of the story containing numerous errors. By focusing attention on the story, this procedure reduced recognition of the tone sequences to chance levels. Despite this, the subjects had a significant preference for those tone sequences to which they had been exposed. Zajonc (1980) reviewed a number of other experiments which point to dual systems of feeling and thought. Subsequent experiments by Seamon *et al.* (1983a, 1983b, 1984) also demonstrated that affective judgments can be made in the absence of recognition.

Zajonc (1980) reviewed the phylogenetic basis for separate cognitive and affective processing by the human brain:

Affect was there before we evolved language and our present form of thinking. The limbic system that controls emotional reactions was there before we evolved language and our present form of thinking. It was there before the neocortex, and it occupies a large proportion of the brain mass in lower animals. Before we evolved language and our cognitive capacities, which are so deeply dependent on language, it was the affective system alone upon which the organism relied for its adaptation. The organism's responses to the stimuli in its environment were selected according to their affective antecedents and according to their affective consequences. (pp. 169-70)

Zajonc concluded that it is likely the brain has two somewhat independent systems for responding to environmental stimuli:

When nature has a direct and autonomous mechanism that functions efficiently - and there was no reason to suppose that the affective system was anything else - it does not make it indirect and entirely dependent on a newly evolved function. It is rather more likely that the affective system retained its autonomy, relinquishing its exclusive control over behavior slowly and grudgingly. At most, the formerly sovereign affective system may have accepted an alliance with the newly evolved system to carry out some adaptive functions jointly. (p. 170)

MacLean's neurophysiological research findings are obviously congruent with Zajonc's conclusions. I have already noted MacLean's conclusion that the limbic brain is geared toward self-preservation and the preservation of the species and operates on the basis of feelings or emotions rather than cognition.

In summary, the research findings I have outlined in the preceding paragraphs *suggest* that: (1) there are dual perceptual systems involving both the uniquely human and the more primitive parts of the brain; (2) the more primitive parts of the brain function on the basis of emotion rather than cognition; (3) the primitive brain can respond to stimuli in the absence of cognitive awareness of those stimuli; and (4), consequently, affective response to stimuli may under some circumstances occur separately from cognitive knowledge. These findings also suggest that 'biological' responses to landscape - based on innate patterns of emotional behavior - could possibly occur quite separately from 'cultural' responses based on learned cognitive patterns of behavior (*cf.* Ulrich, 1983, 1986). This is not to suggest that all or even most experience of landscape involves dual independent systems of response. The point is only that there seem to be dual perceptual systems which may have a bearing on aesthetic experience.

I have already argued that it makes sense to distinguish between the biological and the cultural due to their distinct developmental origins and processes. This approach would be useful analytically even if all behavior involved some amalgam of the biological and the cultural. The evidence suggesting there may be distinct biological and cultural modes of aesthetic experience adds further support to the argument that the biological and the cultural should be addressed separately in landscape aesthetics research. In the pages that follow, however, I use the terms 'biological mode of experience' and 'cultural mode of experience' to refer primarily to the analytical distinction between innate and learned behavior rather than to the distinction between behavior stimulated by limbic system perceptions and that stimulated by cortical perceptions. It would be premature at this time, given the state of knowledge of the matter,

**Table 3** Modes of aesthetic experience and their manifestations as aesthetic constraints and opportunities

| Modes of aesthetic experience | | Constraints and opportunities |
|---|---|---|
| Biological | ———————————▶ | Laws |
| Cultural | ———————————▶ | Rules |
| Personal | ———————————▶ | Strategies |

to speculate further about limbic versus cortical perceptions and their relevance to landscape aesthetics.

## Aesthetics as a System of Constraints and Opportunities

The tripartite theory of aesthetics that I have outlined can usefully be viewed as a system of constraints and opportunities (Table 3). Meyer (1979) developed a general theory of style that is expressed in terms of biological, cultural and individual constraints on behavior as well as opportunities for creativity. As Meyer observed, his theory is applicable to human behavior generally even though, as a theory of *style*, it is oriented to the arts. However, given this orientation, it offers some insights that are particularly relevant to aesthetic theory.

Meyer defined style as 'a replication of patterning, whether in human behavior or in the artifacts produced by human behavior, that results from a series of choices made within some set of constraints' (p. 3). He defined three levels of constraints: laws, rules and strategies. Laws are defined to be transcultural constraints, while rules are transpersonal but intracultural. Strategies are 'compositional choices made within the possibilities established by the rules of style' (p. 27). This definition is obviously oriented to the artist; however, it can be extended to include all personal choices. These three levels of constraints can be applied readily to landscape aesthetics. Laws, rules and strategies can be viewed as manifestations of the biological, cultural and personal modes of aesthetic experience, respectively.

Given this tripartite framework, it follows that the task of theory in landscape aesthetics is one of identifying aesthetic *laws*, if they exist, and identifying the general characteristics or types of aesthetic *rules* and *strategies*. Since rules and strategies are likely to be quite variable, there is more to be gained with respect to theory by identifying their general characteristics and types than by cataloguing them. The study of particular rules and strategies may lead to an understanding of their general characteristics. The fact that rules and strategies are variable leads to the important question of how they are changed. This is where creativity and originality manifest themselves in the personal mode of aesthetic experience. The personal mode of landscape aesthetics is concerned not only with strategies as constraints, but also with opportunities for developing new strategies and new rules. Thus the research agenda with respect to the personal mode could quite productively focus on theories of creativity and their application to landscape aesthetics. This will be the emphasis of Chapter 6, which is concerned primarily with personal strategies as they transcend biological laws and cultural rules.

Research on the biological mode of aesthetic experience could begin with the theory set forth by Appleton in *The experience of landscape* (1975a). Admittedly, this area of research is highly speculative and there is a serious risk of attributing behavior to plausible genetic causes when in fact the behavior is cultural in origin. Appleton's basic thesis is that a landscape that appears to facilitate survival is one that will also provide aesthetic satisfaction. But, as Gould (1980) warned, the fact that behavior facilitates survival does not necessarily mean it is the result of natural selection. Thus the ideas reviewed in Chapter 4 are included in that chapter not because they prove the existence of a biological mode of aesthetic experience, but rather because the authors cited have asserted that their concepts support a biological basis for landscape aesthetics. Furthermore, the theoretical possibility that there is such a mode of aesthetic experience merits including those ideas here. If Appleton's theory were a correct description of a biological basis for landscape aesthetics, then it would describe an aesthetic *law*.

Research on the cultural mode of aesthetic experience could consider, for example, the thesis put forth by Costonis in his article 'Law and aesthetics: a critique and a reformulation of the dilemmas' (1982) and more recently in his book *Icons and aliens: law, aesthetics, and environmental change* (1989). Costonis advanced a 'cultural stability-identity' theory of aesthetics that maintains aesthetic values are reflections of groups' desires to maintain stability and protect their identities. If correct, this theory explains the existence of aesthetic *rules*, *i.e.*, the transpersonal but intracultural bases for aesthetic behavior. Costonis' theory will be discussed in detail in Chapter 5 along with a summary of the literature on cultural variations in landscape tastes. Using that summary as a base, a preliminary typology of aesthetic rules will be proposed.

# CHAPTER 4
# BIOLOGICAL LAWS

The tripartite framework for aesthetic theory set out in the previous chapter suggests a logical division of aesthetic constraints and opportunities into biological laws, cultural rules and personal strategies. As a practical matter, however, it is not at all obvious which aspects of aesthetic behavior are biological, cultural or personal. Much aesthetic behavior probably involves a complex interplay of the three modes of behavior. Furthermore, it is clear that each mode of behavior influences the others. The biological constrains the cultural, which in turn constrains the personal. On the other hand, cultural change can stem from personal innovation, and modifications in the human genome can result from innovations in cultural practices. Indeed, it is not at all difficult to imagine how a trait could begin in the form of a personal idiosyncrasy, be adopted later by a culture, and ultimately result in biological change. For example, some chain of this sort may have led to the genetic change referred to in the previous chapter that allows many adults in Northern Europe and East and West Africa to digest milk.

In spite of the apparent difficulty - and the potential pitfalls - of attempting to sort out the biological, the cultural and the personal, such an effort is a logical means of analyzing landscape aesthetics as a basis for later synthetic applications to practical problems of landscape evaluation and design. Chapters 7 and 8 are devoted to such applications. While those applications are in many ways tentative, I believe they demonstrate the utility of the analytical approach undertaken in this chapter and the two following.

For the purposes of this chapter, *biological laws* will be used to refer to patterns of aesthetic behavior that could be based on a genetic substratum common to *homo sapiens*. The theories reviewed in this chapter have been set forth as 'biological' by their proponents. Thus I am not proposing any new biological theories; I am merely compiling, reviewing and elaborating upon theories that have been proposed by others. As I pointed out in Chapter 3, there is no direct evidence of a genetic basis for aesthetic behavior. In other words, no one has identified specific genes or groups of genes in some way 'responsible' for landscape preferences. Consequently, the evidence that I shall be discussing is indirect and highly speculative, and much more detailed study will be required before any discussion of the biological roots of landscape aesthetics can be anything more than suggestive. What follows, therefore, is not a discussion of laws so much as a review of theories which, if correct, would constitute laws.

## Habitat Theory

What is fairly certain, however, is that a biological aesthetics must be geared toward survival, whether of the individual or the species. Aesthetic preferences must be for landscapes that *appear* to enhance survival. This, in a nutshell, is the assumption underlying Appleton's (1975a) biological theory of aesthetics. Appleton's aesthetics relies heavily on Dewey's assertion that man obtains aesthetic pleasure from satisfaction of basic drives shared with animals. Appleton argues that the environmental implications of these basic drives are fundamentally the same for both man and other animals. For example, self-protection requires an environment that facilitates activities such as hiding, escaping or fighting whether one is human or animal.

Appleton's basic contention is that an environment appearing to offer satisfaction of biological needs is one that will elicit a spontaneous positive response in man that parallels similar instinctual responses in animals. Thus Appleton proposed:

that aesthetic satisfaction, experienced in the contemplation of landscape, stems from the spontaneous perception of landscape features which, in their shapes, colours, spatial arrangements and other visual attributes, act as sign-stimuli indicative of environmental conditions favorable to survival, whether they really *are* favorable or not. This proposition we can call *habitat theory*. (p. 69)

Since Appleton set forth his proposal, Butzer (1977) and Isaac (1980) have examined in some detail the characteristics of the landscapes inhabited by prehistoric man and Orians (1980, 1986), Woodcock (1982) and Wilson (1984) have explored the implications of early human habitats for modern landscape preferences. In summary, these writers argue that for most of his existence man has been a hunter of large game in savanna or savanna-like environments, consisting of grass and isolated trees or groups of trees. Also, there has consistently been a need to remain fairly close to bodies of water because humans need a constant supply of fresh water. These facts seem to provide a plausible explanation for modern man's apparent desire to create parklike landscapes and to live in view of water when given the opportunity.

According to Butzer, 99.8 percent of human existence was prehistoric. Evidence for toolmaking *homo* dates from as far back as the end of the Pliocene (the last epoch of the Tertiary period), about 1,800,000 years ago. The widespread Acheulian material culture of the mid-Pleistocene (the first epoch of the current, Quaternary period), dating from as early as 1,500,000 before present (b.p.) in Africa and continuing in Africa and western Europe until about 200,000 and 100,000 b.p., respectively, displays tools used for hunting and butchering large game. The environmental preferences of these early humans (usually *homo erectus*) were quite consistent:

A survey of the known sites from Africa, Europe, and Asia . . . shows an underlying preference for open, grassy environments, with large herds of gregarious herbivores. The modern environments of such sites range from deserts to forests, but study of their geological context indicates that semiarid or subhumid macroenvironments prevailed at the time of occupancy. Such sites range from what were tropical savannas in equatorial East Africa to what were montane grasslands in glacial-age Spain. This argues that temperature conditions were much less important than was a rich and relatively dependable supply of game. (Butzer, 1977, pp. 579-80)

Isaac (1980) observed that the hominid ancestors of the early humans occupied environments similar to those preferred by the Acheulians. According to the archaeological evidence, none of those environments included dense, unbroken forest, and all included open grassland. Almost all the sites included bodies of water.

The earth's climate became cooler during the Pliocene and Pleistocene, and repeated glaciation destroyed temperate forests in the middle latitudes. Tropical Africa, where man's earliest ancestors developed, was relatively unaffected by the climatic changes, but the glaciation and deforestation in the mid-latitudes allowed expansion of large herbivores and, consequently, the Acheulian hunter-gatherers into Europe and Asia. The Acheulians seem to have avoided deserts and rainforests, even in the low latitudes, due to the relatively low animal biomass available to them in those environments. Woodcock (1982) asserted that the reforestation of Europe that followed the end of the last glaciation resulted in a significant decline in population. It was only during the Holocene (the most recent epoch of the Quaternary, dating from about 10,000 b.p.) that man began to adapt to woodland environments. At the same time, however, agriculture was developed, substituting a man-made savanna or parklike landscape for the natural one. And, as Woodcock (1982) observed, it is only within the past few generations that a significant part of human population has inhabited urban landscapes. Man has for some time modified the landscape with fire while hunting and also to encourage a savanna-like biome. Jones (1975) cited evidence of the widespread use of fire by the Australian Aborigines as a means of both driving game and increasing the usable biomass of the land. For example, the Tasmanian Aborigines in some places replaced a rainforest habitat which provided only marginal subsistence with a quite rich complex of scrubs, heaths and plains. The flora of western Tasmania, for example, indicated a long period of frequent burning prior to the decimation and removal of the Tasmanian Aborigines by European settlers last century:

In 1827, the explorer Henry Hellyer, pushing his way through dense rainforest in northwest Tasmania, climbed to the top of a tall mountain . . . and from there he saw to his delight large open grasslands, extending southwards amongst the rainforest. These plains, which he named the Hampshire and Surrey Hills in memory of the grassy downs of his native England, were the resorts and hunting grounds of the Aborigines, who regularly burnt the grass as they hunted or travelled across them . . . By 1835, all the Aborigines had either died or had been removed . . . and soon afterwards it was noticed that the plains were becoming filled with sour grass and light scrub so that it was becoming difficult to graze sheep on them, the attempt being abandoned with great financial loss about 10 or so years later. (Jones, 1975, p. 26)

Apparently, the Tasmanian form of landscape management has been used by Aborigines throughout the Australian continent. As an example of more recent practice, the Gidjingali of the north of Arnhem Land in northern Australia systematically burn the country surrounding their camp, leaving untouched only areas with edible species of vegetation that would not regenerate readily after fire. According to Jones, 'The main reason given by the Gidjingali for this programme of burning was in order to "clean up" the country, a block of unburnt grassland being regarded rather as we would regard an untidy room' (p. 25).

Basing their arguments on the facts that most of human existence has been in a savanna or parklike biome and that it was evolutionary adaptive for humans to prefer such a habitat, several researchers have suggested that some kind of innate preferences for such an environment may continue today. Orians (1980), cited three types of evidence which suggest this might be the case. These are: (1) the perceptions of explorers in the North American West; (2) the determinants of land prices in free market economies; and (3) the characteristics of designed landscapes. In regard to the first, he noted that explorers seem quite consistently to prefer savanna-like

**Plate 17**   Eugene von Guérard, *Ferntree gully in the Dandenong Ranges*

landscapes with groups of trees, views of water, and vantage points such as cliffs and bluffs, which would all facilitate survival for a large game hunter who wanted to avoid large carnivores himself. Orians noted that in Western literature generally there seems to be a preference for such landscapes and an antipathy to closed forests and bare plains or deserts. In landscape painting, too, there seems to be a focus on the types of landscape that habitat theory suggests would be preferred. Exceptions to this include paintings such as Eugene von Guérard's *Ferntree gully in the Dandenong Ranges* (Plate 17) and Isaac Whitehead's *Gippsland* (Plate 18). Both these paintings depict the interior of fairly dense forests and seem to derive much of their interest from the unusual vegetation depicted. The ferntrees of von Guérard's painting and the huge gums of Whitehead's are particularly remarkable examples of Australian flora. On the other hand, John Glover's *The River Nile, van Dieman's Land* (Plate 19) depicts a more open forest landscape that is, in its general features, a type of landscape not unlike the ones inhabited by early humans. Indeed, the landscape appears to be quite suitable for human habitation: two Aborigines are fishing in the river and another has just caught a possum in the tree to the right of the

**Plate 18**  Isaac Whitehead, *Gippsland*

painting. Admittedly, some of the appeal of this painting is due to the (unrealistic) sinuousness of the eucalypts, a stylistic peculiarity of Glover's.

Explorers in Australasia displayed landscape preferences consistent with those that would be predicted by habitat theory. I have already cited a reference to Hellyer's reaction to the grasslands in northwest Tasmania after he made his way through the relatively inhospitable rainforest. Shepard (1969) noted that English settlers in New Zealand consistently preferred parklike landscapes that reminded them of England. Smith (1979, 1989) cited numerous examples from the works of explorers and early landscape painters in Australia display-ing an attraction for such landscapes. J.W. Lewin's *Two kangaroos in a landscape* (Plate 20) shows what could be characterized as the archetypal Australian parklike landscape, complete with game. According to Smith (1989), even a man like Barron Field, who disliked the mountain scenery and evergreen trees of Australia, was 'able to react with genuine enthusiasm to the gentle curves and blue distances of the savannah lands beyond the mountains, for they brought to mind pastoral imagery deeply woven into the texture of

**Plate 19**   John Glover, *The River Nile, van Dieman's Land*

European poetry and painting – and they represented potential pastoral wealth' (p. 242). But accounts such as this suggest a cultural basis for the appeal of the savanna landscape. Indeed, the accounts by American explorers cited by Orians could reflect acquired landscape tastes just as well as, if not better than, they might reflect innate preferences.

There is some evidence, however, that such preferences might be innate rather than learned. Balling and Falk (1982) conducted an empirical study of preferences for five different types of natural landscape – tropical rainforest, desert, savanna, temperate deciduous forest and coniferous forest. The subjects for the study were mostly from the eastern United States, although a few were university students in Arizona. The subjects included groups of third-, sixth-, and ninth-grade children, university students, professional foresters, biology teachers, retirees and other adults. They rated a set of twenty slides (four of each biome) on a six-point scale ranging from extremely desirable to extremely undesirable. Subjects rated each slide twice, once with respect to the scene's attractiveness as a place in which to live and once with respect to its appeal as a place to visit.

Plate 20   J.W. Lewin, *Two kangaroos in a landscape*

Considering the overall responses of all of the groups, the savanna and deciduous and coniferous forests were preferred as places to live and visit, although their ratings as places to visit were higher than their ratings as places in which to live. The preference for savanna is consistent with the earlier findings of Rabinowitz and Coughlin (1970) and Ulrich (1977), whose subjects displayed a preference for parklike landscapes. In a study similar in some ways to that of Balling and Falk, Woodcock (1982) compared preferences for savanna, hardwood forest and rain forest. In Woodcock's study, subjects were asked to rate sets of slides and the results were analyzed using two clustering algorithms that led to distinctions between open country and forests and between relatively dense and relatively open forest. Preferences were for savanna and then open forest, with dense forest being the least-preferred landscape type.

Using factor analysis, Balling and Falk found that the five biome categories selected for their study did not correspond precisely to psychological categories. With respect to the data on preferences for places in which to live, factor analysis reduced the five biomes to four types: open forest/savanna, desert, jungle and dry savanna. These factors seemed to relate to the openness and aridity of the landscapes, with open forest/savanna preferred overall. With respect to the data on preferences for places to visit, factor analysis reduced the data to the following four categories: desert, forest, jungle and savanna. In this case, the preferred type included only the least arid savanna scenes; the dry savanna scenes were grouped in the least preferred category together with the desert scenes.

The value of the findings reported by Rabinowitz and Coughlin, Woodcock, and Balling and Falk is somewhat limited because the subjects in each case included only Americans. However, the results are consistent with habitat theory, because they demonstrated a decided preference for the type of landscape in which prehistoric man evolved. Balling and Falk's findings are the most conclusive with regard to the innateness of preferences for parklike landscapes. They found a significant correlation between age of the subject and preference, and that the third- and sixth-graders had a decided preference for the savanna biome relative to the deciduous and coniferous forest biomes. The differences in preferences for the three most popular biomes were not significant for any other age groups. The authors concluded that this suggested there is a strong, innate preference for a savanna landscape that is subsequently displaced somewhat by an acquired preference for other types of landscape, in this case deciduous and coniferous forest. This displacement may occur as subjects became more familiar with the deciduous and coniferous forest landscape. Lyons (1983), however, implied that children's preferences for savanna landscapes may be a function of the parklike environments in which they typically play and, therefore, learned rather than innate.

Orians' second type of evidence in support of a biological basis for landscape aesthetics consists of his observation that properties with views and properties adjacent to bodies of water consistently yield higher prices than comparable properties without views or access to water. While preferences for views and proximity to water are consistent with habitat theory, there is no reason why these could not be culturally based. The fact that these preferences seem to be universal does not support the assertion that they are innate.

Orians' third type of evidence is at best only suggestive. He argued that landscape designs of various cultures all seem to seek to create some kind of savanna-like environment. Following Orians, Wilson (1984) noted that the Japanese garden, for example, reflects a 'savanna gestalt' in both its general configuration and the similarities between the shapes of some of the trees used and African acacias. Whether or not the Japanese garden does in fact

Plate 21   Howard Ashton, *Centennial Park*

reflect a 'savanna gestalt' is perhaps subject to debate, but it seems fairly non-controversial to suggest that the English park and its derivatives (including the American suburban yard) do conform to habitat theory. A good example of this is illustrated in Howard Ashton's painting of Sydney's *Centennial Park* (Plate 21). In any case, it seems that the history of landscape design does not provide any salient counter examples that do not conform with the predictions of habitat theory. It is not even clear that there could be any significant counter examples, since they could be explained away as cultural aberrations. All this suggests it is probably not terribly useful to look at the characteristics of designed landscapes as possible evidence of a biological basis for landscape aesthetics.

**Prospect-Refuge Theory**

Appleton (1975a) articulated his habitat theory by focusing on the importance of 'the ability to see without being seen'; he labels this portion of his thesis *prospect-refuge theory*. The relationship between habitat theory and prospect-refuge theory was outlined as follows:

Habitat theory postulates that aesthetic pleasure in landscape derives from the observer experiencing an environment favorable to the satisfaction of his biological needs. Prospect-refuge theory postulates that, because the ability to see without being seen is an intermediate step in the satisfaction of many of those needs, the capacity of an environment to ensure the achievement of *this* becomes a more immediate source of aesthetic satisfaction. (p. 73)

Prospect-refuge theory describes a mechanism that protects individuals from hazards, a third type of environmental feature that plays an important role in Appleton's schema. The ability to see without being seen is particularly important both in pursuing prey and avoiding predators, two important biological needs of early man.

Prospect-refuge theory, with its emphasis on three broad categories of environmental stimuli, served as the focus of most of Appleton's *The experience of landscape*. As Crawford (1976) commented, it is rather odd that Appleton should emphasize the importance of prospect and refuge to the exclusion of other landscape features relevant to biological survival, such as the availability of fresh water. Some of these other landscape characteristics relate to the basic need for information about the environment. With respect to man's information needs, it has been suggested that coherence, legibility, complexity and mystery are all desirable features of landscapes. I will be discussing this *information-processing* approach to landscape aesthetics at some length in the following section of this chapter. Access to prospects contributes to one's ability to efficiently collect information about one's surroundings. There is, therefore, some overlap between prospect-refuge and information-processing theory. The important point is that the prospect-refuge theory can at best explain only part of the biological basis for landscape aesthetics.

Appleton devoted a chapter to categorizing the basic imagery and symbolism of the prospect, the hazard and the refuge, and he further developed this framework by discussing surfaces, light and darkness, levels of symbolism, and scale and locomotion. Light and darkness, for example, were associated with prospect and refuge, respectively. The discussion of levels of symbolism and scale both support the argument that aesthetic response to landscape needs as stimuli only symbols of prospects, refuges or hazards; the real thing is not required. Locomotion was discussed as an important aspect of the aesthetic experience of landscape because it is crucial for survival.

Appleton also devoted a lengthy chapter to illustrating his theory with examples of landscapes as evoked in various art forms. Illustrations were chosen from landscape design, architecture and urban design, painting, poetry and prose. All these examples were carefully selected to support his theory of 'hide-and-seek aesthetics', as he called it. For example, he noted that aesthetic preferences for particular urban landscapes seemed to support his prospect-refuge theory; well-designed pedestrian areas have the characteristic of 'affording the observer the security of lateral cover until the moment when he is ready to concede the refuge as the price of achieving a wider prospect' (p. 196).

Unfortunately, much of Appleton's elaboration of the prospect-refuge theory seems misguided. In developing his 'framework of symbolism', Appleton merely listed and categorized various landscape features. Many of those features are ambiguous symbols of prospect, refuge or hazard (Bunkśe, 1977; Bergman, 1978). Bunkśe noted, for example: 'Darkness may not always signify a refuge, but may instead be forbidding; it is, in fact, one of the few universal environmental elements that induces fear in infants' (p. 151).

Despite his simplistic pigeonholing of landscape elements, Appleton has made a significant contribution to the theory of landscape aesthetics. An unresolved problem, however, is how to further articulate prospect-refuge theory and, more generally, habitat theory. Since these theories refer to biological or innate patterns of behavior, one approach would be to attempt to ferret out the contents of the collective unconscious – the archetypes – which Jung (1959) defined as patterns of instinctual behaviour. Jung suggested several means for identifying the archetypes, including dreams, the products of the active imagination, and other evidence such as paranoiacs' delusions.

Of these types of evidence, the products of the active imagination would seem to be the most accessible. Bachelard's *The poetics of space* (1969) provides an excellent source of poetic images of habitat and refuge. Bachelard devoted chapters to analysis of images of the house, nests, shells, corners, drawers, chests and wardrobes, as well as topics such as 'house and universe' and 'the dialectics of inside and outside'. Consider, for example, Bachelard's account of Henri Bachelin's childhood reveries:

Henri Bachelin's childhood home could not have been simpler ... The lamplit room where, in the evening, the father read the lives of the saints – he was Church sexton as well as day-laborer – was the scene of the little boy's daydreaming of primitiveness, daydreaming that accentuated solitude to the point of imagining that he lived in a hut in the depth of the forest. For a phenomenologist who is looking for the roots of the function of inhabiting, this passage in Henri Bachelin's book [*Le serviteur*] represents a document of great purity. The essential lines are the following (p. 97): 'At these moments, I felt very strongly – and I swear to this – that we were cut off from the little town, from the rest of France, and from the entire world. I delighted in imagining (although I kept my feeling to myself) that we were living in the heart of the woods, in the well-heated hut of charcoal burners; I even hoped to hear wolves sharpening their claws on the heavy granite slab that formed our doorstep. But our house replaced the hut for me, it sheltered me from hunger and cold; and if I shivered, it was merely from well-being'. . . . In this passage from Bachelin's book, the hut appears to be the tap-root of the function of inhabiting. (pp. 30-1).

The aesthetic appreciation of the refuge corresponds with the intensity of the dialectical relationship of the refuge with the prospect or hazard. The pleasure afforded by the boy's hut reverie was enhanced by imaginary wolves scratching at the door. Much of the appeal of the hut-in-the-woods genre of landscape painting seems to stem from the relationships between the primitive refuge epitomized by a rude hut and potential hazards of the surrounding forest. Nicholas

**Plate 22**  Nicholas Chevalier, *The Buffalo Ranges*

Chevalier's *The Buffalo Ranges* (Plate 22) carries this theme even further, combining the picturesque homeliness of a hut at the edge of a forest with the sublimity of overbearing mountains.

Landscape painting provides numerous examples that, like poetry and prose, may contribute to an understanding of the archetypal basis for a biological theory of aesthetics. Appleton illustrates his book with numerous well-known paintings. A few lesser-known examples from Australia may demonstrate the relevance of landscape painting. The refuge imagery provided by the car window frame in Simons' *Emus, Tower Hill* (Plate 2; see page 6) is certainly a major contributor to the aesthetic quality of that painting. The emus would seem much more formidable, and the painting less congenial, without the protective enclosure of the automobile. Eugene von Guérard's *From the verandah of Purrumbete* (Plate 23) and John D. Moore's *Sydney Harbour* (Plate 24) both use the dialectic of prospect and refuge. In the case of von Guérard's painting, the refuge imagery is almost necessary, because it converts an otherwise banal scene into a view of great interest. Moore's painting would perhaps be successful without the window frame, but its appeal is

**Plate 23**   Eugene von Guérard, *From the verandah of Purrumbete*

greatly enhanced by that refuge symbol. The dialectical relationships of refuge and hazard are well-illustrated by Conrad Martens' *Fall of the Quarrooilli* (Plate 25). The casual posture of the two spectators – particularly the reclining one – at the edge of the precipice demonstrates the significance of the proximity of hazard for the appreciation of sublime scenery. The rock outcropping that serves as the spectators' refuge appears precarious while at the same time it is in fact certainly secure. As Burke (1958) observed, the sublime can be appreciated aesthetically only when there is no real danger.

These examples from works of the active imagination show how Appleton's thesis can be developed. Another means of elaborating habitat and prospect-refuge theory is to consider the writing of keen observers of landscape. Carlson (1977) referred to such individuals as 'environmental critics' and I shall refer to them as 'landscape critics'. J.B. Jackson is an excellent landscape critic whose works contain observations that help to articulate Appleton's thesis. For instance, Jackson (1970) described Grand Central Terminal in terms that emphasize not only the sensory experience of the building's interior, but also the dialectic of refuge and prospect:

**Plate 24**   John D. Moore, *Sydney Harbour*

New York City offers a conspicuous example of a rich and almost completely satisfactory sensory experience: Grand Central Terminal. It is entirely proper to analyze its interior as formal architecture or (what is today more fashionable) as an organization of space for certain collective activities, and in any final appraisal of the building those two aspects have to be included. But to the average man the immediate experience of Grand Central is neither architectural not social; it is sensory. He passes through a marvelous sequence; emerging in a dense, slow-moving crowd from the dark, cool, low-ceilinged platform, he suddenly enters the immense concourse with its variety of heights and levels, its spaciousness, its acoustical properties, its diffused light, and the smooth texture of its floors and walls. Almost every sense is stimulated and flattered; even posture and gait are momentarily improved. Few other cities can offer such a concentration of delights; certainly Paris has nothing comparable. The nearest equivalent is the Vienna *Hofburg* with its succession of open places and dark arcades, its tremendous panorama of city and mountains abruptly alternating with intimate architectural areas. (p. 83)

Other, similar examples are discussed by Hiss (1987, 1990), who looked at both Grand Central Terminal and Brooklyn's Prospect Park, designed by Vaux and Olmsted. Speaking of Prospect Park, Hiss described the 'spectacular' transition from the entrance to the

**Plate 25**   Conrad Martens, *Fall of the Quarrooilli*

park through the tunnel called Endale Arch to the extended vista of the Long Meadow one encounters after emerging from the tunnel. To these one might add another American example – the southern approach to central Pittsburgh. Traveling along the expressway from the airport, one enters the Fort Pitt Tunnel through Mount Washington without any preview of the downtown skyline. Exiting the tunnel on the north side of Mount Washington, one is suddenly confronted with a magnificent view of the Pittsburgh central business district on the opposite bank of the Monongahela River. This sudden switch from the dark enclosure of the tunnel to the bright panorama of the city center must be one of the most breathtaking examples of prospect and refuge in America.

Cullen's *Townscape* (1961) includes a discussion of the contrast between what he calls 'hereness' and 'thereness', a distinction that seems much the same as the one between refuge and prospect. His description of the 'enclave' also parallels Appleton's concepts, while emphasizing the dialectical relationship of prospect and refuge:

The enclave or interior open to the exterior and having free and direct access from one to the other is seen here as an accessible place or room out of the main directional stream, an eddy in which footsteps echo and the light is lessened in intensity. Set apart from the hurly-burly of traffic it yet has the advantage of commanding the scene from a position of safety and strength. (p. 25; cited by Appleton, 1975a, p. 197)

Wilson's (1987) discussion of the aesthetics of Italian piazzas echoes Cullen's analysis. According to Wilson, 'because Italy's streets are generally narrow and dark, the piazza should be an explosion of light and space, glimpsed at the end of a street, framed if possible by an arch' (p. 41).

There have been several attempts to test prospect-refuge theory, a number of which are reviewed by Appleton (1984). One of the more noteworthy attempts is the study by Woodcock (1982), already mentioned. According to Woodcock, the findings of his study of savanna and forest biomes are quite consistent with prospect-refuge theory:

In brief people prefer landscapes which provide good views of large expanses of territory with other promising vantage points visible in the distance. But they also prefer that their broad expanses come equipped with convenient refuges as well; they do not favor open spaces devoid of cover. And they like scenes that not only show much but show further opportunities for exploration as well. (p. 302)

Woodcock also found there was a significant difference between the preferences of men and women, with men oriented more to prospects and women more to refuges. This conforms with the different roles of men and women in hunting and gathering cultures and may represent an evolutionary adaptation. Nasar et al. (1988) found a similar difference between men's and women's landscape preferences. Porter's (1987) study of preferences for countryside landscapes found that females gave significantly lower scores to open scenes. Like those of Woodcock, the findings of Rabinowitz and Coughlin (1970) are consistent with prospect-refuge theory. Rabinowitz and Coughlin found a pattern of preference for both 'openness' and 'seclusion' and noted that 'on several occasions, the same site was praised by the same judge for both qualities' (p. 85). Subjects preferred open scenery with clumps of trees or bushes - i.e. parklike scenes combining prospects and refuges - rather than densely forested landscapes.

Two other tests of prospect-refuge theory - by Clamp and Powell (1982) and Nasar et al. (1988) - are relatively limited in scope and inconclusive. The study by Clamp and Powell used 40 panoramas, each consisting of six scenes projected onto a circle of six screens. Four judges (including the authors) viewed each of the panoramas from within the circle and rated the scenes for nine factors, including landscape quality, prospect, refuge, hazard and prospect-refuge balance. There was a significant degree of agreement among the judges about landscape quality, but relatively less agreement about the other factors; and few significant correlations between judgments about landscape quality and assessments regarding the other factors.

The Nasar *et al.* study reported the results of surveys of students at two different locations on a university campus. One location was described as having an open view and the other as having a closed view (although this is not evident in the photographs reproduced in the paper). Students were surveyed at both unprotected and protected observation points at each location. The results indicated that males generally felt safer than females and that the open view was safer than the closed one. Males preferred the unprotected viewpoints, while females preferred the protected ones. As in the case of the Clamp and Powell study, it is not clear that the Nasar *et al.* research says much about the validity of prospect-refuge theory, although (as I have already mentioned) the relationship discovered between sex and preference suggests a possible elaboration of the theory.

**Information-Processing Theory**

Aside from Appleton's prospect-refuge theory, the most significant biologically-based theory in landscape aesthetics is the information-processing theory set forth by the Kaplans (see *e.g.* R. Kaplan and S. Kaplan, 1989), a team of environmental psychologists. Early humans could not have succeeded as big game hunters on the African savanna by means of physical prowess alone; humans must use their wits to a much greater extent than other animals in order to survive (S. Kaplan, 1972, 1973, 1976). As a consequence, humans have developed an ability to acquire and process large amounts of information about their environment. By the same token, they *must* do so in order to survive. The basic contention made by the Kaplans is that environments facilitating and stimulating the acquisition of knowledge will be preferred because such environments were essential to human survival and it is adaptive to prefer an environment conducive to survival. Information-processing theory is clearly a form of habitat theory, and it helps to round out Appleton's overemphasis on prospect and refuge. As I have already mentioned, there is some overlap between information-processing theory and prospect-refuge theory to the extent that prospects are appealing because they help information gathering.

The Kaplans' early speculations on information-processing theory seem to have been stimulated significantly by Wohlwill's (1968) study, focusing on the role of complexity as a stimulus for exploration of both the everyday environment and modern non-representational paintings. Wohlwill's study also related stimulus complexity to preferences for environments and paintings. He hypothesized that exploratory activity would increase with complexity and that the relationship between preference and complexity would be an inverted U-shaped function.

Wohlwill used color slides of places and paintings that were rated for complexity by a panel of judges. Then 28 subjects viewed the slides first to measure the number of times each subject wanted to be exposed to each slide (to test exploratory activity) and secondly to rate the slides for preference. The results confirmed his expectations for both the environmental and the art slides; however, he concluded that exploratory activity and complexity might also be related by an inverted U-shaped function not revealed in this study because the slides did not include extremely complex examples.

One problem with Wohlwill's study noted by S. Kaplan, R. Kaplan and Wendt (1972) is that it does not properly take into account the content of the environmental scenes. The natural scenes used in the study tended to have low complexity, while the urban scenes tended to have high complexity. Thus, what was interpreted as a function of complexity may have been in fact a function of content. To test this, Kaplan *et al.* conducted a study using a series of 56 slides of scenes ranging from urban to natural, with the distinction between the two categories depending largely on the amount of vegetation in the scene. A group of 88 female college students rated the slides, revealing a strong preference for the nature slides. While there was no significant overall correlation between complexity and preference, there were such correlations within each of the nature and urban categories. In each case, complexity was positively related to preference. The authors noted that the backgrounds of the subjects (whether from urban, suburban, or rural or small town environments) did not account for their preferences or ratings of complexity. They also noted the lack of extreme values of complexity in the slides, which may have made the relationship between preference and complexity appear more simple than it actually is.

In any case, the Kaplan *et al.* study demonstrated that complexity *per se* is inadequate as a predictor of environmental preference. This led to a search for other variables and also an attempt to relate the variables to an information-processing theory of landscape aesthetics. Just as Appleton's prospect-refuge focused unduly on only a subset of the many factors affecting aesthetic preference, so does information-processing theory emphasize only some of the possible

Table 4 The Kaplans' preference matrix

| Information outcomes | | |
| --- | --- | --- |
| Timing | Understanding | Exploration |
| Immediate | Coherence | Complexity |
| Inferred, predicted | Legibility | Mystery |

Source: S. Kaplan, 1987, p. 12, Table 1.

biological bases for aesthetics, not to mention the fact that it ignores cultural and personal modes of aesthetic experience. In their book, *The experience of nature* (R. Kaplan and S. Kaplan, 1989) – which sums up about twenty years of research by themselves and their students and colleagues – the Kaplans admitted that information-processing theory is incomplete. It should be noted that they do devote a chapter to group differences in preferences: what I refer to as cultural differences. The Kaplans noted that: 'recognition of differences among groups and differences between experts and non-experts is vital if one is to design and maintain natural settings for diverse users' (p. 73). Nevertheless, there is no attempt on their part to provide a complete theoretical framework for landscape aesthetics.

Information-processing theory has undergone several iterations in various publications by the Kaplans (see *e.g.* S. Kaplan, 1975, 1979, 1987; R. Kaplan and S. Kaplan, 1989). All of these iterations include a two-dimensional matrix that categorizes certain key landscape characteristics according to the manner in which they provide information or encourage the acquisition of additional information. One dimension of the matrix involves a distinction between the information outcomes of understanding and exploration; the other dimension involves the question whether the information is immediately available or predicted or promised (Table 4).

As might be expected, complexity is one of the key landscape characteristics; the others are coherence, legibility and mystery. Complexity is defined as a characteristic that is immediately apparent and that encourages further exploration and study of the scene. Coherence is also immediately apparent, but it is significant because it enables understanding. Legibility and mystery both concern inferred or predicted information, but legibility contributes to understanding while mystery leads to further exploration. Legibility suggests that one will be able to understand the landscape and orient itself; mystery implies there is additional information that could profitably be acquired. Sali Herman's *Sydney 1942* (Plate 26) is a good example of

**Plate 26**   Sali Herman, *Sydney 1942*

the use of mystery in landscape painting: one wants to walk down the alley to see the rest of the boat and the scene beyond.

According to the Kaplans, the four landscape characteristics in the preference matrix are related to preference in different ways. Summing up the results of numerous empirical studies by themselves and their colleagues and students, they observe that preferences seem to be for scenes with mystery and for legible parklike scenes. Some coherence and complexity seem to be required for a scene to be preferred; however, the greater the legibility and mystery, the higher the preference. Furthermore, they noted that the results of studies using regression analyses of the elements of the preference matrix support the conclusion that: 'Mystery is the most consistent of the informational factors' (p. 66).

Some possible interpretations of these results are that too much coherence may lead to boredom and too much complexity may tax one's cognitive abilities. On the other hand, legibility as defined by the Kaplans would always seem to be a good thing; mystery, in suggesting the availability of additional information, does not necessarily imply an overabundance of information being presented simultaneously. Additional information in the landscape may in many cases be discovered at one's own pace, whereas complexity is defined by its immediacy.

Why mystery should be preferred to legibility is unclear, although perhaps the promise of new information is more appealing to a knowledge-hungry creature than the mere assurance that one will be able to orient oneself in the landscape. In any case, one further task of information-processing theory is to explain more fully the relationships between the four informational factors and preference. One step in that direction is Gimblett, Itami and Fitzgibbon's (1985) study of mystery. These authors set out to answer two questions: (1) Can people perceive mystery in the landscape according to the Kaplans' definition? and (2) Which physical attributes of landscape contribute to mystery? To attempt to answer these questions, 191 photographs from a rural site were presented to 36 landscape architecture students. Using multi-dimensional scaling of the results, the authors found there was a high degree of agreement among the respondents regarding the identification of mystery. Also, five physical attributes were found to be associated with mystery; these were screening, distance of view, spatial definition, physical accessibility and 'radiant forest'. The first of these concepts is somewhat vague, and the illustrations included in the paper (Figs. 1 and 2, p. 90) do not clarify matters. Distance of view is negatively related to mystery, while spatial definition or enclosure and physical accessibility in wooded scenes are positively related to mystery. Radiant forest referred to 'wooded areas where the immediate foreground is in shade and an area further in the scene is brightly lit' (p. 92); radiant forest is also positively related to mystery. Gimblett *et al.* correctly noted that: 'At the present time the relationship of the physical attributes to each other and their joint relationship to mystery simply is not clear' (p. 90). Also unclear is the relationship between these attributes and the various other factors affecting landscape preferences.

Like the Kaplans' information-processing theory, Humphrey's (1980) biologically-based theory of aesthetics is structuralist because it emphasizes the relations among landscape elements rather than individual elements. Humphrey's theory focuses on the human desire to understand through classification and can be viewed as an elaboration of aspects of the coherence and, perhaps, legibility components of the Kaplans' preference matrix. Humphrey claimed that: 'Beautiful "structures" in nature or in art are those which facilitate the task of classification by presenting evidence of the "taxonomic" relations between things in a way which is informative and easy to grasp' (p. 63; *cf.* Orians, 1986). According to Humphrey, we like to classify things and we are therefore attracted by rhymes, rhythms and variations on a theme. Nature and the natural landscape are full of such rhythms and variations. The urban landscape must similarly appeal to our desire to classify by providing rhythms and variations that are stimulating but not inscrutable.

## Gestalt Theory

Up to this point, all of the biological theories reviewed were subsumable under the basic concept of habitat theory. Indeed, it is difficult to imagine how any biologically based theory of landscape aesthetics could not be a type of habitat theory. In other words, it is hard to comprehend why preferences for specific types of environments would evolve unless inhabiting those environments would contribute to survival. Gestalt theory, however, is a biological theory of aesthetics which – as it has been formulated to date – is not compatible with habitat theory. Gestalt theory has been applied to architecture (Levi, 1974; Arnheim, 1977) and landscape design (Arnheim, 1966) and therefore merits some discussion here as a theory of landscape aesthetics.

Stated very simply (for more detailed accounts, see Arnheim, 1949; Köhler, 1969; Lang, 1987), Gestalt theory hypothesizes an *isomorphism* between certain formal aspects of environmental objects and neurological processes. Köhler stated this hypothesis as follows: 'Psychological facts and the underlying events in the brain resemble each other in all their structural characteristics' (p. 66). Although there is some recent empirical evidence which seems to support the idea of isomorphism (e.g. Von der Heydt et al., 1984; cf. Gregory, 1977), a theoretical question that arises immediately pertains to the evolutionary basis for such organizational processes. Why should the brain be programmed to react in some specific way to certain abstract formal qualities of the landscape – such as order or complexity – in the absence of any functional basis for such reactions? Gestalt theory offers no answers to such questions, although this is not to say that answers do not exist.

One of the primary concerns of Gestalt theory is the manner in which objects are distinguished in a visual field or, in other terms, the manner in which figures are distinguished from ground. The ability to separate figure and ground obviously affords evolutionary advantages, but it is not clear that an explanation of this process would have any direct implications for landscape preferences. It is possible that Gestalt theory could make some contributions to information-processing theory, particularly to the understanding of the operation of coherence and legibility, but this possibility has not yet been explored.

One problem with Gestalt theory is that it has been applied normatively by environmental designers even though it provides no basis for the assumption that formal Gestalt qualities – such as simplicity or unity – are aesthetically preferable. Gestalt theory obviously suffers from the same problem as formalist theory, generally. Scruton's (1979) comment on formalist theory applies with equal force to Gestalt theory: 'it does not really capture the *meaning* which it purports to analyze' (p. 66). Thus, the fact that Gestalt theory is not a form of habitat theory is a very clear indication of its inadequacy as a biological explanation for landscape aesthetics; it does not purport to *explain* anything. The Gestalt psychologist Kanizsa (1979) admitted that 'today gestalt theory does not have much credit as an explanatory theory' (p. 3).

The theories of Appleton, the Kaplans and Humphrey are pioneering efforts toward identification of possible biological bases for landscape aesthetics. Unlike Gestalt theory, each of these theories fits within the scope of habitat theory, because each involves speculation about evolutionary mechanisms which led humans to be attracted to environments conducive to survival – *i.e.* good habitats. Obviously, as has been suggested, these theories are incomplete. Where, for example, does the need for access to fresh water – which might explain much of the appeal of bodies of water – fit into these schemes? Admittedly, the Kaplans (R. Kaplan and S. Kaplan, 1989) note that there are a number of content-based categories – such as water or nature – that are highly preferred, but these observations are not integrated into or related to their basic theoretical framework. Much work, both speculative and experimental, remains to be done. Because the work that has been done to date is at best suggestive, it would be premature to attempt to make applications to the problem of landscape evaluation and design. Thus, any applications suggested in Chapters 7 or 8 will be extremely tentative.

# CHAPTER 5
# CULTURAL RULES

In Chapter 3, I stated that rules were transpersonal but intracultural. Rules are those bases for behavior that are transmitted socially rather than genetically. Because they are transmitted socially, rules are manifested in the activities of groups of people rather than single individuals. I am using the term *group* to refer to a set of individuals sharing some common characteristics. However, groups can be defined by biological characteristics as well as cultural characteristics, so it must be recognized that not all groups are cultural groups. This means that the aesthetic preferences displayed by groups may be reflections either of biological laws or cultural rules and that group preferences should not be assumed to be either biological or cultural preferences. What distinguishes cultural preferences is the fact that they are transmitted socially; if transmission occurs socially, then a preference is culturally-based.

It should be clear that I am using the term *culture* in what Merquior (1979) referred to as the 'historicist-anthropological' rather than the 'humanistic' sense. While the latter is evaluative and concerned with ideals, the former is simply 'empirically given'. In this chapter, therefore, the focus is on aesthetic preferences as they *are* rather than as they *should be*. To some extent, the latter question will be addressed in Chapter 6, where I shall discuss the role of personal creativity in changing cultural rules. Normative aesthetics will be considered even more directly in Chapter 7, which is concerned with landscape evaluation and criticism.

It should also be noted that the concept of cultural rules does not imply anything about the size of the group manifesting those rules. The group in question could be as small as a family, for example, or as large as the Orient. Indeed, it is quite possible that some 'cultural' attitudes and behavior will be shared by as few as two individuals and that others will be shared by all humans. What is important is not the size of the group, but the fact of social transmission.

## Cultural Identity and Stability as a Basis for Cultural Rules

The cultural basis for behavior – including aesthetic behavior – is transmitted socially through the use of language and other tools. These means of communicating culture are symbolic in nature. Indeed, the identities of cultural groups are achieved symbolically. There would be no culture without symbolic systems to represent that culture. Thus it is not surprising that philosophers such as Cassirer (1944) and Midgley (1978) have emphasized the use of symbols as the most distinguishing feature of human culture. Midgley elaborated on that theme with her observation that human culture is also characterized by habit. In other words, culture not only seeks its identity in symbolic forms, but it also seeks to maintain itself through such forms. The landscape is one form through which cultural groups seek to create and preserve their identities (Duncan, 1973; Appleyard, 1979; Rowntree and Conkey, 1980).

It is also not surprising that a cultural theory of landscape aesthetics should emphasize both symbol and habit. Costonis' (1982, 1989) 'cultural stability-identity' theory does just that. Costonis' theory is strictly a cultural theory, as it does not address the possibility of a biological basis for aesthetics. This is somewhat surprising in view of his repeated references to Dewey's *Art as experience* (1934), which presented a strong, clear argument in support of a biological foundation for aesthetics. Nevertheless, Costonis' theory is quite convincing as an explanation of the nature of cultural rules. Costonis does to some extent address the personal basis for aesthetics, but does so in a way that confounds the personal with the cultural, as will become evident in the following paragraphs.

Costonis approached the subject of aesthetics as a legal theorist, and he was concerned with the theoretical bases for aesthetic jurisprudence. In this context, he was interested in the theories that could support controls on the aesthetic aspects of land development. Costonis examined two competing theories. One was the 'visual beauty' hypothesis, which refers to a desire to preserve or create a visually beautiful environment. The visual beauty hypothesis assumed there are some sensory or formal attributes of the environment that are inherently attractive and therefore warrant protection. Following Dewey, Costonis observed that the concept of 'beauty' has no analytical content and he rejected the 'visual beauty' hypothesis as a meaningful explanation of aesthetic value. Costonis preferred the 'cultural stability-identity' hypothesis, which finds a basis for aesthetic controls in the desires of groups to protect their identities by exercising control over their environments. It is evident that this hypothesis directly addresses the fundamental characteristics of human culture as identified by Midgley.

According to Costonis (1982):

It is true, of course, that viewers respond affirmatively to particular visual configurations in the environment. Their responses, in fact, are often suffi-ciently patterned to refute the objection that aesthetics is too subjective to warrant legal protection. But these configurations are compelling because they signify values that stabilize cultural, group, or individual identity, not because their visual qualities conform to the canons of one or another school of aesthetic formalism. (pp. 357–8)

In arguing against aesthetic formalism, Costonis stated that aesthetic response is comprised of reactions to symbolic, non-sensory aspects of the environment as well as to the environment's sensory attributes. These symbolic features of an object include: 'the *meanings* ascribed to it by virtue of our individual histories . . . and our experiences as members of political, economic, religious, and other societal groups' (p. 399). In response to the formalists' asser-tions that beauty can be defined in terms of the formal character-istics of objects, Costonis pointed out that, even if this were the case, no one has found any satisfactory rules for identifying formal beauty. If Costonis had considered the possibility of a biological basis for aesthetics, he may not have completely rejected formal aesthetics. Within the context of a cultural theory of landscape aesthetics, however, it does seem appropriate to discount formal aesthetics and give more attention to symbolic aesthetics – emphasizing the interaction of subject and object rather than the one-sided objectivism of formalist theory. Any theory of cultural aesthetics must take into account the attitudes people bring with them to the landscape. These attitudes can vary from group to group and can change with time. Costonis argued that the simplistic objec-tivism of formal theory was inadequate: 'We do not so much *discover* aesthetically compelling properties in the environment . . . as *ascribe* them to it on the basis of our individual and cultural beliefs, values, and needs' (p. 401).

Costonis referred to the circumstances of actual aesthetic contro-versies in support of his argument that the symbolic aspects of the landscape are more important than any canons of visual beauty. As an example, Costonis discussed a dispute regarding the preservation of the Isaac L. Rice Mansion in New York City's West Side. In that case, a mansion was threatened with demolition and replacement with a 30-story tower. The architectural quality of the mansion and the proposed tower were barely considered in the course of the controversy which led to the mansion's protection through designa-tion as an historic landmark. Instead, opponents of the tower 'reacted ... to the *idea* of the tower as associationally dissonant with the Mansion on the West Side' (pp. 393-4).

An example from Philadelphia supports similar conclusions. In 1982, a developer proposed to build a fourteen- or fifteen-story glass-faced office building in the Rittenhouse Square area of central Philadelphia. In order to do this, he would have had to demolish three turn-of-the-century houses. In response to the developer's proposal, some eighteen organizations grouped together and formed the Rittenhouse Preservation Coalition which, among other things, published a 24-page report on the problem, organized a community meeting attended by several hundred neighborhood residents, and helped to draft a zoning amendment that protected the threatened buildings and surrounding blocks (Foglietta, 1983; Frey, 1983).

Here, as in the case of the Rice Mansion controversy, the issue was largely aesthetic: the threatened buildings and the landscape of which they are a part are a source of a consummatory, or inherently meaningful, experience, to use Dewey's term. But although the community's concerns were largely aesthetic, the issue was not primarily a matter of visual beauty; instead it was the community's way of life that was at stake. It seems unlikely that more than a few of the neighborhood's residents had any specific knowledge of the threatened building's architectural or historical significance before the controversy arose. But this lack of knowledge in no way prevented the development of a widespread negative reaction to the developer's proposal. A letter to the editor of a local newspaper, written by the president of the Center City Residents' Association (which was active in the Rittenhouse Preservation Coalition), stressed the relative importance of preserving the community's quality of life (Halpern, 1983). In reference to the re-zoning which protected the site from redevelopment, the letter stated:

This zoning change enhances the prospects for the preservation of the buildings [threatened with demolition] as well as the fine federal-era buildings ... and the Victorian houses within the area. *More important, it protects the present blend of highrise buildings, commercial store fronts and fine residential houses which makes Center City such a fine area to live and work.* This vibrant environment is an attractive, exciting home for a heterogeneous population of professionals, artists, business people, older citizens and families. *These people have a stake in the quality of life in town* ... (my italics).

This example, like that of the Rice Mansion controversy, provides clear support for Costonis' theory.

The importance of symbolism in cultural attitudes toward landscape is demonstrated by the fact that even the labels one attaches to landscapes can have significant impacts on preferences for those scenes. Hodgson and Thayer (1980) showed that photographs of land-scapes were consistently ranked lower when labeled with terms implying human influence. Using two identical sets of fifteen photographs, these authors varied the labels on four scenes. In one set, the four scenes were labeled with the terms 'lake', 'pond', 'stream bank' and 'forest growth'. In the other set, the same scenes were identified as 'reservoir', 'irrigation', 'road cut' and 'tree farm', respectively. Three groups of subjects from different places in California each had significantly lower preferences for the scenes labeled with terms implying human influence. In a similar vein, Buhyoff *et al.* (1979) found that knowledge of the presence of damage by southern pine beetles has a significant negative impact on preferences for forest scenes.

Rowntree's (1981) interpretation of historic preservation efforts in Salzburg, Austria, sums up the significance of cultural symbolism for landscape aesthetics. Rowntree noted that preservation objectives reflect 'visual neighborhood biases' and that: 'Since landscape tastes are nurtured by traditional scenery, the connection with historic preservation becomes obvious: people tend to preserve the familiar' (p. 62). And: 'In an era of rapid environmental change, visual biases and aesthetic traditions are used to slow landscape transformation ... Landscape tastes, it would seem, reflect the biases of a people toward the artifacts of their occupancy by giving cultures a sense of historical perspective and identity through their surroundings' (p. 62).

## Consistencies and Variations in Cultural Rules

The cultural stability-identity hypothesis is not a cultural rule; instead, it explains the existence of cultural rules. In other words, it is a theory of the cultural foundation for aesthetic rules. As I stated in Chapter 3, my purpose in this chapter is not to catalogue the many varieties of cultural rules, but rather to explain their general characteristics and offer a typology of rules as a useful means of organizing future research efforts. However, as a preliminary step toward that end, it will be helpful to review some of the empirical literature on cultural attitudes towards landscapes. I shall be draw-ing evidence from the growing body of experimental work in land-scape perception and aesthetics. Admittedly, much of this work lacks a sound theoretical foundation and also suffers from problems of methodology and interpretation. For the most part, I shall not dwell on those problems, some of which are addressed in more detail in Chapter 7. Arguably, clues about cultural attitudes might be culled from other sources, particularly artworks such as works of literature and paintings, not to mention folklore (see *e.g.* Bunkśe, 1978). But to work from such a vast, intractable base of material would make the present task impossible. Also, in spite of their problems, the experimental data are probably more directly suited to my purposes.

Before discussing research identifying variations in cultural values, it is appropriate to review those studies that have suggested or attempted to demonstrate that such variations in landscape preferences are insignificant. Coughlin and Goldstein (1970), for example, found there was a high level of agreement among a panel of judges about the aesthetic quality of suburban and rural scenes near Philadelphia. Although the authors report that the judges on the panel had a range of backgrounds, no specific details are given and one is left wondering whether there were in fact any significant differences among the judges to support an hypothesis of heterogeneous aesthetic values. Shafer and Tooby (1973) also failed to explain why one should expect any differences between the two populations they studied: campers in American campgrounds and Scottish campgrounds. They reported a very high positive correlation between the preferences of campers in America and Scotland for photographs of natural landscapes. There is no reason, however, to expect that the two groups would display any fundamental differences. As Porter (1987) observed, the two cultures probably have more similarities than differences in their general reactions to natural landscapes.

Similar problems are evident in studies by Zube and Mills and Ulrich. Zube and Mills (1976) assessed the preferences of three sets of subjects for photographs of the shoreline of Lorne, Australia. The subjects were: (1) year-round residents of Lorne; (2) seasonal residents and non-residents; and (3) American landscape architecture students. There were high correlations among the responses of all three groups. As in the case of the Shafer and Tooby study, these results are not surprising, since there is no apparent reason for divergent attitudes toward beach scenery among the three groups studied.

Ulrich (1977) used photographs of roadside scenes from Michigan in a comparison of the aesthetic preferences of residents of Michigan and Sweden, finding a high positive correlation between the results for the two groups. He did, however, find some minor differences between the two groups – Americans tended to give higher ratings to certain scenes with smooth, mowed surfaces. Ulrich attributed this to Americans' exposure to mowed lawns and roadsides; in contrast, most Swedes live in apartments, do not maintain lawns and their roadsides are less likely to be mowed. Here again, there is no apparent reason why the *general* preferences of Swedes and Americans should differ, so a demonstration that they do not does not really say much about the importance of cultural values in landscape aesthetics.

A final set of studies involved inter-regional and cross-cultural studies of preferences for photographs of Rocky Mountain and Appalachian Mountain scenes. Wellman and Buhyoff (1980) compared the preferences of students from Utah (who were familiar with the Rockies) and Virginia (who were familiar with the Appalachians) for scenes from the two mountain ranges. There were no significant differences between the preferences of the two groups and the authors concluded that: 'This is one piece of evidence, then, which suggests that generic landscape preference models may be viable' (p. 110). Again, however, there is no reason to assume that the residents of Utah and Virginia might have different attitudes toward two types of mountain scenery.

Another problem with the Wellman and Buhyoff study is that the Appalachian and Rocky Mountain scenes were apparently so similar that they probably represented generic mountain scenery rather than the distinctive landscapes of particular regions. Describing their methods for selecting photographs, the authors noted: 'The scenes from each region should be relatively similar with respect to such potentially confounding variables as topography, water, evidence of man's influence, seasonality, foreground vegetation and cloud formations' (p. 106). One wonders what was left to distinguish scenes from each of the two regions. Inspection of the actual photographs (reproduced in Buhyoff *et al.*, 1983) fails to dispel skepticism about the methods employed by Wellman and Buhyoff.

A more recent study by Buhyoff *et al.* (1983) used the same eleven photographs and compared the preferences of the original American subjects (aggregated into one group) with the preferences of groups of subjects from the Netherlands, Sweden and Denmark. In this case, there was no hypothesis that preferences for Appalachian scenes might differ from those for the Rocky Mountain scenes. The results showed fairly high correlations between the preferences of observers in Denmark and the Netherlands (r = .84) and also for observers in the United States and Sweden (r = .89); the other correlations were relatively low. The authors described the differences between the two pairs of groups: 'Danes and Dutch prefer flat and open landscapes, whereas Americans and Swedes show a higher appreciation of forested and mountainous scenes' (p. 188). They hypothesized 'that these potential biases in preference taxonomies would be the result of cultural influences or familiarity with features of their own environments' (p. 189).

In a study of Asian subjects' preferences for scenes from the Rocky and Appalachian Mountains (using Wellman and Buhyoff's set of photographs), Tips and Savasdisara (1986a) found basic agreement in preferences among subgroups defined in terms of urbanity (*i.e.* residence in rural, rural-urban fringe, or urban areas), travel experience, and 'macro-geographic background' (*i.e.* residence in hilly, mountainous, river valley or flat areas). In a related study, Tips and Savasdisara (1986b) compared preferences for the same set of photographs of various Asian subjects, Western tourists in Asia, and indigenous and ethnic Chinese living in Thailand. The authors found significant correlations among the preferences of each of these groups and also among the preferences of these groups and Buhyoff *et al.*'s (1983) results for Danish and Dutch groups; however, there were few significant correlations between the Asian results and Buhyoff *et al.*'s results for Americans and Swedes.

While the research cited in the preceding paragraphs for the most part failed to find cultural differences in aesthetic values, it is apparent that the groups studied in many cases could be expected to share the same general sets of values – for example, toward mountain or shoreline landscapes. In other cases, the groups studied apparently do not share the same attitudes toward landscapes. For the most part, the studies cited have characterized cultural groups according to nationality. One problem with this approach is that it tends to result in a not very enlightening list of preferences catalogued by nationality.

Race is another questionable means for characterizing cultural groups. While race is essentially a biological characteristic, it is often used as a means for identifying ethnicity. R. Kaplan and Talbot (1988), for example, explicitly used race as a means of identifying members of different cultural groups in their study of differences in the landscape preferences of blacks and whites. The findings that blacks preferred scenes with built elements (*cf.* Zube and Pitt, 1981), smooth ground texture, and well-maintained appearance to a greater degree than whites would seem to be much more subject to cultural than to biological explanation. Race is irrelevant to landscape preferences unless it corresponds to some meaningful cultural group. And, as in the case of nationality, it seems unlikely that listing the preferences of different racial groups will in itself reveal anything systematic about the operation of cultural rules.

Age and sex are also criteria for differentiating cultural groups. The extent to which the behaviors and attitudes of different age and gender groups are culturally rather than biologically determined is sometimes unclear. For example, Lyons (1983) noted there are biological factors that are a function of age and that may affect environmental cognition. On the other hand, differences among different age groups may be cultural phenomena reflecting the effects of varying degrees of experience or maturity or even historical trends manifesting themselves in the form of differences between generations (Dearden, 1989). Lyons' paper reported that young children showed significantly higher preference ratings than other age groups and the elderly significantly lower preference ratings. Young children also displayed greater variation or inconsistency in their evaluations than did other age groups. In a comparative study of the landscape preferences of Eskimo from coastal and inland villages in arctic Alaska, non-native populations from the same areas, students from the University of Delaware, and junior high school students from Delaware, Sonnenfeld (1966) discovered that younger groups preferred more exotic landscapes. Dearden (1984), however, found no statistically significant age-related differences in a study of preferences for wilderness, rural and urban scenes.

As in the case of age, it is not clear whether behavioral differences between sexes are due to biology or to socially-defined sex roles. Some differences between the landscape preferences of men and women were presented in Chapter 4, and there are plausible arguments that these differences might be genetic. However, Lyons (1983) argued that the gender differences she found were probably due to the sex-role differentiation that takes place during adolescence. The only significant sex differences she found were in adolescents and older age groups. Although the results are not discussed in detail, Maciá's (1979) research apparently discovered significant sex differences in preferences for slides of landscapes. Sonnenfeld's (1966) research revealed that males preferred what he called 'subsistence-oriented' and 'rugged' landscapes, while females preferred 'richly vegetated' and 'warmer' landscapes; these differences are perhaps related to the gender differences in preferences for prospect-and refuge-oriented landscapes discussed in Chapter 4. On the other hand, Dearden's (1984) study revealed no significant sex-related variations in preferences, although there was a tendency for females to prefer urban scenes more than males did.

The question of whether a group's behavior is biologically or culturally determined does not arise in regard to most of the other criteria for defining cultural groups. These criteria may be related either to membership in specific social groups or to residence in or some other kind of familiarity with places. The socially-defined criteria include factors such as ethnicity, religion, socio-economic status, occupation, or membership in various groups such as political parties (regarding the latter, see Craik, 1975, 1986). The place-related criteria involve familiarity with specific places or types of places.

Jacques (1980) proposed using socio-economic data as criteria for identifying groups with similar tastes, but he did not provide any substantial support for this recommendation and admitted it would be difficult to define appropriate socio-economic criteria. For example, income or educational level *per se* would not seem to have any direct relationship with landscape preferences. In regard to the latter, it seems clear that education in the design professions would be more significant than education *per se*. In regard to income, while it is true that one's experiences are constrained by one's opportunities, which are themselves constrained by income, it would be more to-the-point to use experience as the relevant variable.

Working from a fairly extensive empirical base, R. Kaplan and S. Kaplan (1989) argued that familiarity is the major factor accounting for differences among groups. They also remarked correctly that familiarity results from experience of places, and that this experience can take different forms such as residing in or visiting a place, or indirect forms such as reading about a place. Familiarity *per se* does not imply anything about one's attitude toward a place (S. Kaplan and R. Kaplan, 1989). Familiarity can breed indifference as well as positive or negative dispositions. For example, Hammitt (1981) found that hikers responded more favorably to photographs of a bog environment after hiking through it than before. Hammitt interpreted his results to mean that direct experience of the bog enhanced preference ratings. Similarly, Keyes (1984) found that hikers along a trail in the Great Smoky Mountains National Park gave higher preference ratings to photographs of the trail after hiking than before.

Dearden (1984) also found some connections between the density of the housing occupied by his respondents and their preferences for certain types of landscapes. The lower the density, the higher the preferences for rural and wilderness (*i.e.* less developed) landscapes. These results do not necessarily say anything about the relationship between familiarity and preferences, because the preferences could have predated and motivated the choice of residential environment. Somewhat more interesting are the data Dearden obtained when he asked his respondents to rank ten potential influences on their landscape preferences. The most highly ranked influences – past landscape experience, travel, present living environment, recreation activities, education and reading – all seem to involve familiarity.

On the other hand, Aoki (1983) found that newcomers gave more favorable assessments of the urban landscapes of Tsukuba Science

City in Japan than did other residents, possibly suggesting that preferences declined with familiarity. Another interpretation would be that longer-term residents had different attitudes toward the City to begin with. Dearden (1984) suggested that 'Respondents could both prefer the familiar over the unfamiliar, and yet rate familiar landscapes lower than newcomers to the region' (p. 295).

Even more ambiguous results are reported by Nasar (1980), who studied the attitudes of groups of residents from two neighborhoods in Knoxville, Tennessee, to photographs both of their own neighborhood and of the other group's neighborhood. As would be expected, residents were more familiar with their own neighborhood. Residents found their neighborhood to be more pleasant than the unfamiliar one but the unfamiliar neighborhood to be the more interesting. (It would have been interesting to combine the pleasantness and interest results into some kind of composite preference rating.) Herzog et al. (1976), in a study of college students' attitudes toward familiar scenes in Grand Rapids, Michigan, found there was a positive relationship between familiarity and preference with respect to certain types of scenes and a negative relationship with respect to others. Scenes of cultural, commercial and entertainment buildings were viewed positively, while scenes of contemporary buildings and, notably, college campus buildings were viewed negatively. Oddly, Herzog et al.'s (1982) subsequent study of preferences for unfamiliar urban scenes ignored cultural factors, addressing only the four components of the Kaplans' preference matrix (see Table 4, page 85).

Pedersen's (1978b) study of the role of familiarity employed 42 university students and a nineteen-item semantic differential test to rate views of forest, beach, small town, desert and large city landscapes. Factor analysis of the results produced four categories, which Pedersen labeled 'evaluation', 'spiritual', 'activity' and 'esthetic appeal'. The distinctions among these categories are not entirely evident. For instance, the 'evaluation' category included factors such as 'nice', 'valuable', 'important', 'clean', 'adequate', 'pleasant', 'comfortable', 'good', 'interesting' and 'stimulating', while the 'esthetic appeal' category included factors such as 'natural', 'beautiful' and 'like'. Pedersen found that only the 'evaluation' category was positively correlated with environmental familiarity at significant levels. Part of the problem with this study is the assumption that familiarity is positively correlated with preference. Another problem is that the results of the factor analysis may be spurious, since there seems to be no clear analytical distinction between the 'evaluation' and 'esthetic appeal' categories (cf. Pedersen, 1978a).

Familiarity is meaningful as a source of cultural aesthetic

attitudes only if one's experience of a place is imbued with some sort of social significance. In the experience of the bog environment cited by Hammitt, the actual experience of the environment presumably resulted in greater knowledge of the place than could be obtained simply by inspecting photographs. While enhanced understanding of a place need not result in a more *positive* attitude toward that place, it may provide a firmer basis for applying one's pre-existing cultural norms regarding such places. Thus the bog hikers, who had favorable attitudes toward the bog before hiking, had even more favorable attitudes afterwards.

Familiarity is closely related to ethnicity to the extent that the latter is tied to specific places. As in the case of familiarity, ethnicity in itself does not imply any particular attitude one way or the other. In a study of preferences for Virgin Islands landscapes, Zube and Pitt (1981) discovered that Virgin Islanders did not think hotels or apartment buildings detracted from the scenic quality of sandy beaches. Other ethnic groups, from the United States and Yugoslavia, perceived such buildings unfavorably, suggesting that they symbolized different things to the different groups. Similarly, Rodie's (1985) study considered the attitudes of various groups to cultural modifications (such as churches, houses, oil tanks and power lines) to countryside landscapes in the Flint Hills region of Kansas. Local rural residents were less disturbed than other groups by the landscape modifications. Rodie concluded:

If the viewer who lives in the countryside has expectations which already include negative elements such as powerlines or oil tanks (much as the urban inhabitant overlooks the continual overhead maze of utility lines), then countryside scenic quality may not be as critical (in theory) to the inhabitants of the countryside as it is to non-regional observers who view the landscape from a different perspective. (p. 91)

Porter (1987) arrived at results – which I shall discuss in more detail in Chapter 7 – analogous to those of Rodie and Zube and Pitt. These results seem to lend some support to Sonnenfeld's (1966) argument that there is a need in environmental planning to allow for the human ability to adapt to deficient landscapes (see Chapter 2). To use Sonnenfeld's terminology, what appears unattractive to the 'non-native' may be acceptable to the 'native' because the latter has had time to adapt to the landscape. It seems more likely, however, that the different preferences of the native and non-native may be due simply to the different symbolic values found in the landscape by these two groups.

A good example of this is given by Kwok (1979) in a paper reporting the results of a cross-cultural study. Kwok's study used 66 semantic differential scales to evaluate fifteen slides of various environments and found differences in the perceptions of residents of Singapore, Sweden and England. For example, scenes of supermarkets are apparently viewed more positively in Singapore than in Sweden, perhaps because supermarkets are a novelty in Singapore and a 'necessary evil' in Sweden. On the other hand, scenes of multistory apartment buildings received relatively low evaluations from Singaporeans, apparently because many of them are forced to live in them.

In a comparison of Japanese and American preferences for urban street scenes, Nasar (1984) concluded that each group of respondents favored scenes from the other group's country more than scenes from their own country. To qualify his findings of a negative relationship between familiarity and preference, Nasar suggested: 'It is possible that extremely familiar scenes would be preferred to others' (p. 272). In a study with results similar to Nasar's, Yang (1988) assessed the attitudes of Koreans and Western tourists in Korea to Korean, Japanese and Western garden styles. The Korean respondents preferred scenes from Japanese-style gardens over scenes from Western-style gardens, and Western-style scenes over Korean ones. The Western tourists also preferred scenes of Japanese-style gardens more than either of the other types; however, their second and third preferences were for Korean- and Western-style scenes, respectively. As Yang suggested, there may be some fundamental characteristics of the Japanese garden that make it more appealing universally; but this would not explain the orders of the second and third preferences of the two groups.

In contrast, studies by R. Kaplan and Herbert (1987, 1988) showed that Michigan university students tended to prefer natural Michigan scenes more than Western Australian university students did. At the same time, the Western Australian students preferred Western Australian scenes more than the Michigan students did. In these cases, familiarity was generally positively related to preference. An exception to that conclusion was found through factor analysis of the results for the Michigan scenes, which revealed that the Australians were relatively unfavorable toward pastoral or open rural scenes. R. Kaplan and Herbert (1988) interpreted this as follows:

It seems likely that while the Australian sample was not directly familiar with any of the scenes included in the study, the genre of the open, rural settings is one they recognize readily. This is probably the most common nonurban landscape in the area near Perth, Western Australia. In this case, a relative sense of familiarity with settings that are not highly preferred seemed to breed contempt. (p. 387)

It is interesting to compare these results with the previously-cited findings of Zube and Mills (1976). Zube and Mills did not find

Plate 27    Russell Drysdale, *Joe's Garden of Dreams*

significant differences between the preferences of Australians and Americans; however, their study focused on the shoreline rather than on vegetation. While Australian flora are quite unique, the shoreline is less distinctive, indicating that familiarity would have a more significant role to play with respect to the former.

While familiarity and ethnicity – to the extent that it is a type of familiarity – do not in themselves imply anything about a group's attitudes toward a landscape or type of landscape, they do have certain broad implications. Familiarity implies a certain kind of knowledge about a landscape that leads the 'insider' to view things differently from the 'outsider'. Consider, for example, the differences between the insider's and the outsider's perception of the scene depicted in Russell Drysdale's *Joe's Garden of Dreams* (Plate 27). In particular, as I have noted in Chapter 2, the insider tends to see things in terms of their practical import, while the outsider sees only the surface. Sonnenfeld (1966) proposed the terms 'native' and 'non-native' to capture what I refer to by 'insider' and 'outsider'. Although Sonnenfeld's terms 'native' and 'non-native' as he uses them are synonymous with 'insider' and 'outsider', the latter terms are preferable to the former because native implies a connection based on birth or origin, while insider does not. It is stretching the definition of native somewhat to say that a non-native can become a native, while it does not offend common usage to speak of an outsider becoming an insider.

There are different kinds of familiarity – not just that of an insider such as a long-term resident who has extended direct experience of a place. There is also, for example, the armchair reader of travelogues who has only indirect knowledge. While the armchair traveler is an outsider, he or she nevertheless has a degree of familiarity with the place or with the kind of place in question. The armchair traveler is, therefore, to some extent an 'expert'. Other types of experts include those professionals – such as architects, landscape architects, planners and resource managers – who are directly involved with landscape aesthetics. Numerous studies have documented similarities and differences between the attitudes of these professionals and their 'non-expert' clients.

Studies demonstrating similarities include those by Fines, Craik, Zube et al., and Dearden. As a preliminary to a study of landscape quality in East Sussex, England, Fines (1968) conducted a limited comparison of the landscape evaluations of three groups defined by: (1) considerable experience in design; (2) limited experience; and (3) no experience. The members of each group were required to evaluate twenty color photographs of various landscape scenes. The rankings produced by the three groups were basically the same, although the range of values increased with experience in design, suggesting that those with such experience could produce finer differentiations among scenes than could those without.

Craik (1972) found similarities between experts and non-experts in their landscape perceptions. Craik compared the responses of experts and non-experts to 50 slides of landscapes. The subjects in this study were required to evaluate the slides along 34 descriptive dimensions and also to assign each of the scenes to one of ten schematic land-scape types. In regard to the descriptive dimensions, there was a significant positive correlation between the responses of the members of each group. There was also substantial agreement in assigning scenes to the schematic landscape types.

Seven groups of subjects participated in Zube et al.'s (1975) study of evaluations of the everyday rural landscape in the northeastern United States. These groups were: (1) professional environmental designers; (2) natural resources students; (3) environmental design students; (4) professional resource managers; (5) technicians; (6) elementary and secondary school teachers and housewives; and (7) secretaries. Each subject made comparative evaluations of pairs of slides from a set of 27 scenes. The correlations among the seven sets of evaluations ranged from .43 to .91, with an average of .77. A study of a subset of the original set of slides using fourteen bipolar semantic scales (such as beautiful–ugly) resulted in even greater agreement among groups, leading Zube *et al.* to conclude there was relatively high agreement between experts and non-experts in this study. Zube's (1984) comparative study of landscape descriptions and evaluations of environmental designers, on the one hand, and resource managers, on the other, found a fairly high level of agreement between the two groups of experts.

Dearden (1984) compared the preferences of planners, Sierra Club members, and urban park users in Victoria, British Columbia. Individuals from each group were asked to evaluate photographs of wilderness, rural and urban landscapes. While the planners and park users had essentially the same preferences - preferring rural, wilderness and urban scenes, in that order - the Sierra Club members gave first preference to wilderness. Dearden interpreted these results to mean that professional training in planning does not have a significant influence on preferences for different landscape types.

On the other hand, Craik (1970) concluded: 'There are plenty of reasons for advancing the hypothesis that environmental decision-makers differ from their clients in their perception, interpretation, and evaluation of the everyday physical environment' (p. 89). Following Lipman, Craik noted the impact of professional training as well as the social and administrative distance that often separates environmental decision-makers from their clients. Lipman (1969) observed that architects tend to be distinct from the users of their buildings in terms of both educational and social backgrounds. This suggests they may not appreciate the behavioral patterns of their clients. Furthermore, 'the intervention of administrative agencies standing between architects and building users' (p. 198) makes it difficult for architects to have any personal contact with their clients. Evidence such as Gans' (1962) study of Boston's West End documents the differing perceptions of the inhabitants of a neighborhood and the planners seeking to 'renew' it. As Gans (1968) noted elsewhere, the planner's perspective is often quite like that of the tourist. Although an 'expert', the planner is too often also an 'outsider'.

An excellent example of this is given by Appleyard (1969), in his report on the planning of Ciudad Guayana in Venezuela. Not only were many of Ciudad Guayana's planners foreigners, but the most important decisions were made by a bureaucracy in Caracas which was both geographically and socially quite remote from the site

(Peattie, 1969, 1987). Sensitive to the different values of the planners and their clients, Appleyard attempted to measure some of these differences by interviewing individuals drawn from various groups in the city. His results revealed that the planner's

motivations are general, diffuse, and future oriented, whereas the inhabitant's are usually particular, specific, and present oriented; his experience with cities is usually much greater than that of the inhabitant, which makes it difficult for him to see or plan with an 'innocent' eye. His familiarity with the city is usually more extensive than intensive, and his information media are so abstracted and amplified with 'objective' data that his world tends to become divorced from the real city. His very abilities and knowledge create the gap. (p. 450)

In their study of natural landscapes, R. Kaplan and S. Kaplan (1989) emphasized the expert–non-expert distinction as well as familiarity. Studies by R. Kaplan, Twight and Catton, and Rodie demonstrate some of the differences between experts and non-experts. R. Kaplan (1973) compared the preferences of 107 students in architecture, landscape architecture and non-design fields. The subjects were asked to rate each of 60 scenes for preference as well as coherence and mystery. Factor analysis of the results revealed three categories: (1) natural scenes; (2) buildings-with-nature; and (3) building complexes. The three groups of subjects differed in their responses to each of these categories. The architecture students had significantly lower preferences for the scenes in the nature category than did the other two groups. They also had significantly higher preferences for scenes in the building category. The landscape architecture students had significantly greater appreciation for the scenes in the buildings-with-nature category, while the non-design students had the lowest mean rating for scenes in that category. The author concluded:

The pattern that emerges from these results is one of strong differences in preference as a function of area of professional interest with an understandable preference for buildings on the part of Architects, a divided preference of buildings and landscaped settings for the Landscape Architecture students, and a strong preference for unadulterated, enclosed nature settings for the College [non-design] students. (p. 270)

Twight and Catton (1975) reported the results of a study of users and managers of the University of Washington's arboretum in Seattle. The managers' perceptions, as revealed by stated goals and operating plans, emphasized scientific, educational and horticultural functions of the arboretum. Users, on the other hand, were 'oriented toward aesthetic and amenity values' (p. 301). A majority of users preferred a pleasant landscape and a restful atmosphere over a variety of plants and flowers. This seems to be a case in which the experts are insiders focusing on the various practical functions of an arboretum, while the non-experts are outsiders concerned mainly with the appearance of the place.

Rodie's (1985) study of the Flint Hills area of Kansas also compared the evaluations of experts and non-experts. He found that landscape architecture students and resource managers tended to be more negative than teachers, Grange members and church members. In particular, resource managers had a significantly lower preference than either teachers or church members for scenes with cultural modifications such as buildings or other structures. In this case, the experts were outsiders, while the non-experts were insiders.

In an interesting pair of studies, Hendee and Harris and Buhyoff *et al.* assessed the ability of experts to gauge the preferences of non-experts. The Hendee and Harris (1970) paper reported the results of a study of wilderness users and managers in the Pacific Northwest region of the United States. The managers were asked to give their estimates of users' preferences as well as their own personal preferences. Ironically, although the managers' personal attitudes were very much like those of the users, their estimates of users' attitudes were, in the authors' judgment, fairly inaccurate. In contrast, the Buhyoff *et al.* (1978) paper reported that landscape architects could accurately predict the preferences of clients even though their own preferences differed from those of the clients. In this research project, 86 non-expert university students ranked nine color slides of southwestern Virginia mountain scenery and also listed those factors which affected their preferences. The expert group consisted of 21 landscape architecture students and faculty members. Eight of the experts had professional design experience, while the balance did not. This group read the factors listed by the non-expert subjects and then ranked the scenes the way they thought the subjects would rank them. Then the experts ranked the scenes according to their own preferences. While there was a high correlation between the subjects' rankings and the experts' estimates of the subjects' rankings, there was no significant correlation between the subjects' rankings and the experts' own preferences. There was, however, a considerable amount of variation among the individual landscape architects' estimates of the subjects' preferences. Furthermore, the landscape architects with professional experience were not able as a group to predict accurately the subjects' preferences. This suggests that professional experience reduces the likelihood that landscape architects will be able to estimate the preferences of their clients.

## A Typological Framework for Further Study of Cultural Rules

My objective in this section is to classify those characteristics of groups that result in systematic variations in aesthetic values. I am not interested in all such characteristics so much as those that have important implications both for further research in aesthetics and for applications to landscape planning and design. What emerges from the research cited in the preceding section is a two-dimensional typological framework with familiarity and expertise as the two dimensions. These two dimensions reflect particularly significant sources of variations in aesthetic attitudes because they are both important sources of problems in landscape planning and design. All too often, the planning or design expert has values quite distinct from those of the people being designed or planned for. This may be due not only to the social and educational background of the expert, but also to the expert's lack of familiarity with the values of his or her 'clients'. Because familiarity and expertise have such important implications for planning and design, they also provide a useful framework for further empirical research in landscape perception and attitudes.

The familiarity and expertise dimensions also subsume significant aspects of many of the other criteria for categorizing cultural groups. For example, it is essentially familiarity that makes nationality, ethnicity and many other societal groups relevant as criteria for distinguishing variations in aesthetic values. Familiarity may even account for some age- and sex-related differences in values. Expertise, on the other hand, captures much of what is consequential about educational level and social class.

One way of characterizing the familiarity dimension is in terms of the insider–outsider dichotomy, or what I shall label 'existential status'. These terms represent a more precise way of conceptualizing the matter because 'existential status' and 'insider–outsider' both refer directly to membership in cultural groups. In contrast, 'familiarity' might be taken to refer to experience of a landscape rather than participation in a cultural group. Since members of different cultural groups can experience the same landscape in quite different ways due to variations in cultural values, it clearly makes more sense to define familiarity in terms of membership in a cultural group rather than experience of a landscape.

The expertise dimension is particularly important when it involves 'expert' professionals who are making decisions affecting 'non-expert' clients. For this reason, I shall label the expert–non-expert dichotomy 'professional status'. The existential and professional status dimensions are arrayed in Table 5, which includes

**Table 5**  A typological framework for cultural groups and rules with examples of cultural groups

|  | Professional status | |
| --- | --- | --- |
| Existential status | Expert | Non-expert |
| Insider | Local planners | Local citizens |
| Outsider | Foreign architects | Most tourists |

examples of cultural groups that might fall in each of the cells of the matrix. Insider, outsider, expert and non-expert all refer to extremes, and specific individuals or groups will fall somewhere between these polar limits. Where a specific individual or group falls obviously depends upon the context as, for example, an architect may be an outsider in one cultural group but an insider in another.

Some applications of the matrix in Table 5 will be considered in Chapters 7 and 8. For example, proper appreciation of the significance of the insider–outsider dichotomy helps to clarify some of the methodological and interpretational errors in the numerous studies purporting to demonstrate that natural landscapes are preferred to urban ones. Also, attention to the problems of existential and professional status can help planners and designers to overcome some of the gaps between themselves and the people who will be inhabiting the spaces they produce.

Culture is defined by persisting symbols, some of which are in the landscape. Once a landscape acquires meaning for a cultural group, that group will seek to perpetuate that symbolic landscape as a means of self-preservation. Aesthetics is a matter of consummatory experiences, and the symbolic landscape provides such experiences for members of the relevant cultural groups. Thus, the role of cultural rules in landscape aesthetics is to define the manner in which different cultural groups find symbolic meaning in the landscape.

While a growing body of experimental literature has attempted to compare the aesthetic preferences of cultural groups defined in diverse ways, it appears that the dimensions of familiarity and expertise – or, more precisely, existential and professional status – capture much of what is most consequential about cultural variations in aesthetic values. Given this two-dimensional framework, it may be possible to carry out cross-cultural research in a more systematic manner.

# CHAPTER 6
# PERSONAL STRATEGIES

Just as it is difficult in many cases to distinguish the biological mode of aesthetic experience from the cultural, it is not immediately obvious what distinguishes the personal mode from the other two. It is helpful to recall Vygotsky's observation (see Chapter 3) that biological and cultural influences come together in ontogenesis, or personal development. Furthermore, it seems it is through intellectual activity that the individual can transcend the biological and cultural constraints on his or her behavior. Vygotsky's model therefore suggests that individuals' personalities should be viewed as composites of biological and cultural constraints and personal idiosyncrasies. In so doing, one must address the phylogenic and sociogenic bases for aesthetic behavior as they come together in ontogenesis. But this approach also forces one to recognize that much of what is commonly referred to as personal or individual behavior is in fact biological or cultural in origin. Behavior which is personal in the *strict* sense is only that which transcends the biological and the cultural. Thus one analytical strategy would be to view the personal mode as that which goes beyond the constraints of biological laws and cultural rules. The focus in this chapter will be on such transcendent behavior.

This approach is not, however, the one taken by most researchers in landscape aesthetics. For example, researchers have studied individuals' 'environmental personalities' (Craik, 1970), 'environmental dispositions' (Sonnenfeld, 1969), 'environmental specializations' (Little, 1975), environmental 'constructs' and 'repertory grids' (Harrison and Sarre, 1971, 1975, 1976), or 'environmental cognitive sets' (Leff, Gordon, and Ferguson, 1974; Leff and Gordon, 1979). The Kaplans (see *e.g.* R. Kaplan, 1977) devised an Environmental Preference Questionnaire and McKechnie (1970) developed an Environmental Response Inventory, both of which were designed to assess individuals' environmental dispositions. These tools permit researchers to relate personality characteristics to environmental preferences. R. Kaplan (1977) found, for instance, that 'The person with an appreciation for the suburbs finds himself realistic in outlook and confident that he can handle a challenge' (p. 212). In a similar kind of study, Maciá (1979) found, among other things, that social extroverts prefer humanized landscapes, introverts prefer natural landscapes, men with mature personalities who deal effectively with reality prefer humanized landscapes, women with sensitive, insecure personalities prefer natural, unaltered landscapes, and so forth.

In view of the tripartite framework set forth in this book, it must be recognized that there are difficult analytical problems involved in this approach to the personal mode of aesthetic experience. For example, the gender differences discussed by Maciá may be biologically-based, culturally-based, or some combination of the two. If culturally-based, they may be applicable only to members of the sampled population – in this case, Spanish university students in the liberal arts. Similarly, the results reported by R. Kaplan might not be generalizable beyond the group of Michigan teenagers from which *her* sample was drawn. Furthermore, these personality differences are quite probably subject to change over time as cultural attitudes change. Working within the context of the Vygotskian paradigm should help researchers to avoid confounding biological, cultural and strictly personal modes of aesthetic experience.

In focusing on the strictly personal mode of landscape aesthetics, it is useful to consider two types of personal strategies. Personal strategies are *perceptual* strategies if they involve ways of perceiving the landscape. In most cases, these ways of seeing will be limited to particular individuals, but sometimes innovative individuals will transmit their perceptual strategies to others, using prose, poetry, painting or some other means of communication. Personal strategies may also be *design* strategies to the extent that individuals are able to incorporate aesthetic innovations in plans or designs for modifying the landscape.

In either case, strategies may be viewed as either constraints or opportunities, to use the terminology introduced in Chapter 3. Personal strategies are the means by which individuals take advantage of opportunities to be innovative. On the other hand, when an innovative strategy becomes an habitual mode of behavior, it must be viewed as a constraint. The terms constraint and opportunity are polar extremes, and most personal behavior (in the strict sense) will fall between them.

What is most interesting about personal strategies from a theoretical point of view is the fact that they presuppose an ability to transcend biological and cultural constraints. Indeed, it seems that changes in cultural rules start out as innovative personal strategies (Barnett, 1953). The important question for theory, then, is this: How do individuals transcend their biological and cultural aesthetic constraints? Or, to say the same thing differently: How does creativity manifest itself in individuals' aesthetic behavior? This chapter seeks an answer to these questions by first reviewing theories of creativity and then applying those theories in a consideration of the role of personal creativity in landscape aesthetics.

**Theories of Creativity**

The most fundamental theoretical question regarding creativity concerns the origin of that which is created. On the one hand, there is the idea that that which is created is totally new and therefore not the product of anything previously in existence. In this view, creative inspiration is a mystical, ineffable process, and there is no point in trying to understand it because it has no antecedents. This opinion was apparently held by some of the creative individuals studied by Barron (1969) and MacKinnon (1962) and their colleagues. One subject (a poet) even wrote an article expounding upon the foolishness of attempting to understand creativity. This view of creativity is also the one contained in the first chapter of the Book of Genesis, in which God creates the world from a void.

But, as Barzun (1989) noted, Genesis is ambiguous in its concept of creation. In contrast with the story in the first chapter, in the second chapter of Genesis God does not begin with a clean slate. Rather, He begins with a dry and lifeless earth and uses it to create new forms. For example, man is produced from dust and woman from man's rib. Here God's act of creation is evolutionary. In this view, creativity is a process that employs existing materials to form the new.

Of course, my subject in this chapter is human creativity and not that of an omnipotent god. The latter could presumably take whatever form desired by the god. Human creativity seems much more constrained by biological laws and cultural rules, as well as by the environmental materials available for manipulation. For example, a painter is constrained by the biological restrictions on the range of light frequencies visible to the human eye. He may be somewhat less constrained by the range of techniques available to painters in the late twentieth century. After all, this is one area in which painters may exercise some creativity. Nevertheless, the available materials are not unlimited, and even if they were, the artist, being a mere mortal, would hardly be able to explore all the possibilities. Analogously, the poet's subject matter is necessarily viewed from a human point of view rather than, say, that of a bird. The poet may try to think like a bird, but he remains a human trying to put himself into a bird's mind. He never actually becomes a bird because biology necessitates that he experience the world from a human perspective. At the cultural level, the poet is constrained foremost by language, although he may be able to modify language or use it in novel ways. One could continue with such examples, but it is evident that, unlike gods, humans cannot create *ex nihilo*.

Furthermore, it seems that everything humans create is some combination of preexisting materials or ideas. Koestler, who wrote what is perhaps the most authoritative tome on creativity, *The act of creation* (1964), emphasized this point. For Koestler, each of the three major domains of creativity – humor, discovery and art – involves what he terms 'bisociation'. Bisociation always consists of a combination of preexisting things. What makes such a combination creative, however, is that it involves *'the perceiving of a situation or idea . . . in two self-consistent but habitually incompatible frames of reference'* (p. 35). Thus the creator is able to see something in a non-traditional way and thereby make something new of it.

For example, consider Franklin's use of a kite to conduct lightning and thereby prove that clouds are electrical bodies (Koestler, 1964, pp. 202–4). One result of Franklin's extensive study of electricity was his belief that clouds were electrified. He hypothesized that iron rods could be placed on houses and other structures to attract lightning and discharge it through wires connected to the ground. He needed to prove somehow that clouds were electrical bodies, however, before he could convince people of the utility of his lightning rods. At first, Franklin thought that the erection of a very tall church spire in Philadephia might allow him to capture the electricity from a cloud, but this proved infeasible. Later, he recalled the days of his youth when he would float on his back on a lake while being towed by a kite. The combination of a kite and a lightning rod was the bisociative act that solved his problem.

For Koestler, creativity can be manifested in biological evolution, cultural changes and personal development. In each case, creativity depends upon 'ripeness': 'We may distinguish between the *biological ripeness* of a species to form a new adaptive habit or acquire a new skill, and the ripeness of a *culture* to make and to exploit a new discovery . . . Lastly (or firstly), there is the personal factor – the role of the creative individual in achieving a synthesis for which the time is more or less ripe' (Koestler, 1964, p. 109). While there are remarkable parallels between Koestler's conception and the tripartite framework set forth in this book, it will be noted that I am treating creativity as an essentially personal phenomena while Koestler seems to be saying it is a process that operates at all three levels of the framework. It is not difficult, however, to reconcile the two views.

As Barnett (1953) demonstrated in great detail, cultural change originates in personal innovation. As Koestler urged, the culture must be 'ripe' to accept a particular innovation, else it will remain a personal idiosyncrasy and nothing more. But, in Barnett's 'socio-psychological' view of culture, innovations must be viewed as essentially combinations of ideas. They must exist as ideas before they can take any material forms. Some innovations are intended to remain ideas and never take any material form. In any case, innovative ideas necessarily take their initial forms in the minds of individuals and are subsequently adopted or rejected by other individuals. If adopted by a significant number of individuals, they result in cultural change. Thus: 'All cultural changes are initiated by individuals' (Barnett, 1953, p. 39).

Biological creativity has its own dynamic even though it is not entirely independent of cultural and personal creativity. Biological creativity is to some significant degree independent because it is influenced by environmental factors unaffected by personal innovation and cultural change. On the other hand, as I mentioned in Chapter 3, it is not hard to imagine how personal innovation could lead to cultural change and then biological evolution. This may explain, for example, why some groups can digest alcohol and lactose while others cannot. Even more significantly, it is not hard to imagine how the vast environmental changes wrought by mankind – all of which were stimulated by personal innovations adopted by ripe cultures – may be affecting the biological evolution of humans. While there seems to be little or no firm evidence of this (perhaps due to the difficulty of sorting out the biological and the cultural), the logic of the argument is compelling.

While cultures *per se* do not create anything, they must be ripe if they are to adopt specific innovations. Ripeness means both that conditions are propitious for creative individuals to make certain innovations and that the culture is poised to embrace those innovations. With this in mind, it should not be surprising that sometimes two individuals independently make an important discovery at the same time. Thus it should not seem odd that Darwin's evolutionary theory was discovered more or less simultaneously by Wallace. Darwin is credited with the discovery only because he did much more than Wallace to develop the idea. Furthermore, as Koestler pointed out, the concept of ripeness explains why the more original a discovery is, the more obvious it seems afterwards: 'The more familiar the parts, the more striking the new whole' (p. 120). How often do we ask ourselves, 'Why didn't *I* think of that?'

Having characterized creativity as originating in personal, bisociative acts, it remains to be determined how individuals are able to achieve such acts. Koestler noted that many creative individuals have stressed the importance of unconscious processes in achieving innovative solutions to problems. Creative individuals seem to be able to retreat to relatively primitive and subconscious processes to enable them in effect to look at things in a non-traditional manner. Thus scientists such as Einstein have relied on visual imagery as a means for solving problems. Koestler observed that '*as vehicles of thought*, pictorial and other non-verbal representations are indeed earlier, both phylogenetically and ontogenetically older forms of ideation, than verbal thinking' (p. 173). Non-verbal modes of thought are useful precisely because language is a source of habit and rigidity in thought patterns. In other words, it is a cultural constraint. Given the tripartite structure of the human brain outlined in Chapter 3, it is not surprising that humans should use the different levels of the brain as a means of viewing phenomena from different perspectives. Indeed, it is interesting to speculate that if the human brain were more unified, humans might be much less creative.

This by no means suggests that creativity is a function solely of primitive brain functions. On the contrary, it is evident that the most creative individuals are those who are most knowledgeable about the problem they are seeking to solve. Koestler provides numerous examples of this from various fields, demonstrating that creative persons are typically primed for creative acts by immersion in the relevant subject matter. Eliot (1957) made the same point with regard to poetry, emphasizing the importance to the poet of being grounded in the history of poetry. According to Eliot: 'No poet, no artist of any art, has his complete meaning alone. His significance, his appreciation, is the appreciation of his relation to the dead poets and artists. You cannot value him alone; you must set him, for contrast and comparison, among the dead. I mean this as a principle of aesthetic, not merely historical, criticism' (p. 49). And Colquhoun (1982) argued forcefully that architects need to have an extensive knowledge of the history of the field in order to be creative in the present. In Koestler's terminology, resort to primitive non-verbal modes of thought will not lead to a bisociative act unless the individual is ripe with materials for bisociation.

**Plate 28**   Jeffrey Smart, *Cahill Expressway*

## The Role of Personal Creativity

I have already remarked that personal strategies may be manifested
in the form of perceptual strategies on the one hand, or design
strategies on the other. Creative perceptual strategies are important
in landscape aesthetics because they may result in changes in
cultural attitudes toward the landscape. Such strategies may show
cultural groups how to appreciate landscapes more fully. A good
example of this is the change in attitudes toward mountain scenery
that took place in the seventeenth and eighteenth centuries. As I
have suggested, for innovative strategies to be adopted by cultural
groups they must be diffused in some way. Examples of this were
discussed in Chapter 1. Monet, for instance, transmitted his perceptions of water lilies by means of his paintings. Another interesting
example of the diffusion of innovative perceptual strategies is the set
of short stories collected by Helen Daniel in *Expressway* (1989).
Each of the stories in that collection was written in response to
Jeffrey Smart's *Cahill Expressway* (Plate 28). The stories add layers

of significance to the scene and, particularly, its solitary occupant. They encourage readers to see Smart's painting from a variety of novel points of view. The matter of perceptual strategies has been addressed quite effectively elsewhere and I will not dwell on it here. Shepard's *Man in the landscape* (1967), Tuan's *Topophilia* (1974), and Tunnard's *A world with a view* (1978) are particularly good sources.

In anticipation of the discussion of postmodernism in Chapter 8, I wish to devote several paragraphs to design strategies. Creative design strategies involve actual changes in the landscape. I argued in Chapter 1 that 'landscape' is the appropriate aesthetic object in both architectural and landscape design. Because it is the whole scene that we experience and respond to, it is not relevant to speak of the aesthetics of individual objects in the landscape (such as buildings) without asking how those objects contribute to the wholes (landscapes) of which they are a part. Thus good design with respect to any segment of the landscape requires careful attention to context. Context here refers to all of the various geographical, historical and other factors relevant to the design problem. Many aspects of context involve only the local situation. Climate, topography, local cultural values, social and political issues, the character of adjacent sites, local building techniques and so forth are all elements of the local situation. Other aspects of context are more universal, such as the designer's knowledge of the history of design, international building techniques, design theory and so on. The best designers will be thoroughly versed in all these areas in order to be primed for a creative act of design.

By defining context broadly, it makes sense to define design as the problem of fitting form to context. This is precisely the definition given by Alexander in his book, *Notes on the synthesis of form* (1966). Alexander's definition

is based on the idea that every design problem begins with an effort to achieve fitness between two entities: the form in question and its context. The form is the solution to the problem; the context defines the problem. In other words, when we speak of design, the real object of discussion is not the form alone, but the ensemble comprising the form and its context. Good fit is a desired property of this ensemble which relates to some particular division of the ensemble into form and context. (pp. 15-16)

This theory of design is clearly congruent with Costonis' cultural stability-identity theory (see Chapter 5). The question whether a change in landscape form will be 'culturally disintegrative' or 'culturally vitalizing' is a question about goodness of fit. In particular, it is a question about the relationship between new form and existing cultural values.

This is not to suggest that good design must necessarily reflect existing cultural values. What it must do, however, is to react to those values in one way or another. Consider, for example, the design of a building. In most cases it is probably appropriate for a building to attempt to conform to its cultural context, assuming there are some meaningful cultural values that could have a bearing on its design. If not, the building may need to try to create a context for other, future buildings. In some cases, it may be appropriate for a building to depart slightly from existing values as a means for influencing a change in them. In other cases, though, it may be appropriate for a building to depart sharply from its context because it has some special symbolic importance.

Meyer's (1979) distinction between two different types of creativity helps to elucidate some of these points. He commented:

> The distinction between rules and strategies helps ... to clarify the concepts of originality – and its correlative, creativity. For it suggests that two somewhat different sorts of originality need to be recognized. The first consists in the invention of new rules. Whoever invented the limerick was original and creative in this sense; and Schönberg's invention of the twelve-tone method also involved this sort of originality. The second sort of originality, on the level of strategy, does not involve changing the rules, but discerning new strategies for realizing the rules. A Bach or Haydn, devising new ways of moving within established rules – or an Indian sitar-player improvising according to existing canons on an age-old raga – is original and creative in this way. (p. 38)

While Meyer's examples are musical ones, his concepts apply equally well to landscape design. Most designs simply involve new strategies for achieving established rules. Only the best designers are able to be so innovative as to successfully change the rules.

Unfortunately, there has been a tendency in twentieth century environmental design to overemphasize the innovative at the expense of traditional – particularly pre-Modern – design values. This aspect of the Modern movement in architecture and design has resulted in an excessive number of unsuccessful attempts at innovation on the part of designers who might have done quite good work if only they had not attempted to be so innovative. One can imagine that if more designers had been content solely to devise strategies for working within traditional design rules, then the typical modern urban landscape would be more cohesive and not such an unsatisfying hodgepodge of meaningless architectural idiosyncrasies. A detailed critique of both modern and postmodern design is provided in Chapter 8.

I emphasized in Chapter 1 that the landscape is a form of art that is imposed on the public. It must therefore be more socially responsible than other art forms, such as painting or literature, which can easily be avoided. This means that environmental designers require much greater discipline, to insure they produce designs that either conform to the existing context or improve upon it or perhaps even create a new context. There is a serious danger, however, that regulation of design will stifle desirable innovation, whether in the form of new strategies or new rules. Public control of design, therefore, should involve a careful balance between the need to protect communities from designs that do not conform to their contexts, while at the same time providing opportunities for creative innovations that may lead to constructive changes. This is by no means an easy task, but characterizing the problem of design review in this way is at least one step in the right direction.

From an analytical point of view, it is most useful to view personal strategies as those aspects of personal behavior that transcend biological and cultural constraints. Of course, if personal strategies become habitual modes of behavior then they constitute another form of constraint. The focus in this chapter has been on strategies as opportunities for creative behavior. Creativity has been characterized as essentially personal, although a culture must be 'ripe' if an individual's innovation is to flourish. Creation involves what Koestler has termed a 'bisociative act', which means the creator is able to see something in a non-traditional manner. Creative individuals are apparently those who can look at things in non-traditional ways, thereby breaking out of habitual modes of thought. At the same time, however, the individual creator must also be 'ripe' in order to recognize a creative solution to a problem. This means the creative individual must be very knowledgeable about the various aspects of the problem to be solved. This applies to both creative perception and creative design. In regard to the latter, the designer must be steeped in the context of the design problem. It is only in this manner that the designer will be prepared to create a form that fits well within its context, to use Alexander's terms.

# CHAPTER 7
# LANDSCAPE EVALUATION

This and the following chapter are intended to demonstrate some applications of the ideas contained in the preceding chapters. In this chapter I am concerned primarily with showing how the theory of landscape aesthetics could be used to inform the practice of landscape evaluation, particularly the debate regarding quantitative evaluation techniques. For this purpose, I have selected several examples of quantitative techniques, including a relatively primitive model, which appeared fairly early on in the current spate of literature on landscape evaluation, and two more sophisticated approaches. After using these examples to illustrate some of the limitations of quantitative evaluation techniques, I then conclude the chapter with a recommendation that landscape evaluation conform to a model that I call *landscape criticism*.

The ideas presented in the preceding chapters have a number of general implications for quantitative evaluation techniques. One of the more important implications is the need to be explicit about the distinctions between biological laws, cultural rules and personal strategies and how these phenomena might operate with respect to the landscapes being evaluated. A brief example will demonstrate what I mean. Researchers such as Ulrich (1979, 1981) have made much of the apparent fact that humans seem to prefer so-called 'natural' scenes over urban ones. Simple comparison of 'preference scores' for natural and urban scenes seems to provide clear quantitative evidence in support of Ulrich's conclusion. As Zube (1974) remarked, however, this kind of research may involve the comparison of apples with oranges. The tripartite paradigm suggests why Zube may be correct. It is possible that natural landscapes are experienced more in the biological mode (*i.e.* with respect to their values as potential habitats) and urban landscapes more in the cultural mode (*i.e.* with respect to cultural symbolism). I do not mean to discount the significance of cultural factors for natural landscape preferences. Attitudes toward mountain scenery, for example, are clearly cultural phenomena. It is likely, however, that different sets of cultural values apply with respect to different types of landscapes. Thus, the types of elements that might make a natural landscape attractive could be rather different from – and perhaps incommensurable with – the factors that would make an urban landscape appealing.

Furthermore, all humans probably share some innate preferences for certain types of natural landscapes (*e.g.* savanna), but preferences for urban landscapes may depend to a greater extent upon membership in a cultural group for which those landscapes hold some meaning. Perhaps a more serious problem is the fact that many of the urban scenes used in preference studies probably hold no particular significance for *any* cultural group, much less the groups represented by the individuals surveyed in those studies. Ulrich (1981) explicitly attempted to factor out much of the potential cultural significance in his urban scenes: 'To ensure that the scenes were not generally familiar to the individuals participating in the study, no slides were taken in the city of Lund or its immediate vicinity, the area where the subjects lived' (p. 527). And: 'The urban scenes primarily depicted commercial landscapes, and to a lesser extent industrial areas. They excluded residential areas, churches, funeral agencies, police stations, fire stations and hospitals, because of the possibility that emotional associations would bias the results' (p. 528)! But if 'emotional associations' are to be factored out of the study, then something is clearly missing from the theoretical model underlying Ulrich's study. What is missing is an understanding of the role of cultural symbolism.

The cultural mode of experience is not the only one that is often neglected in quantitative landscape evaluation methods. These methods also usually fail to allow for the possibility of cultural change or, in other words, they do not address the personal mode of experience, particularly the role of personal creativity. Personal creativity is relevant in landscape evaluation in a number of respects. For instance, creative individuals may be able to see value in a landscape that may not be appreciated by the general public for one reason or another. In this case, it may be appropriate to give more weight to the evaluation of the creative individuals than that of the general public, in view of the possibility that the public may in time come to appreciate the landscape. Here, one would be unnecessarily foreclosing the possibility of desirable change by assuming that existing values were fixed.

It is also relevant to recall that creative individuals are necessarily well-grounded with a thorough knowledge of their subjects. Thus the landscape expert should have some understanding or insight that would not be expected on the part of the general public. The expert should, for example, be able to explain how a landscape was in the past, how it came to be the way it is, how it functions today and what it is likely to become in the future. The expert should also be able to read and interpret the layers of cultural meaning in the landscape and assess their significance vis-à-vis other cultural values, social, political and economic issues, and so forth. All of this is to suggest that the expert may be able to enlighten the public and thereby change landscape perceptions and attitudes.

Another major implication of the theory presented in the preceding chapters concerns the limitations of formalist, objectivist approaches to landscape aesthetics. Quantitative evaluation techniques focus on formal qualities of the landscape because such qualities can be measured in quantitative terms much more readily than, say, symbolic aspects of the landscape, which are intangible. (In view of this, it is not surprising that quantitative techniques tend to focus on natural rather than urban landscapes due to the difficulty of developing any meaningful quantitative measures of the latter.) Given the problems with formal and objectivist aesthetic theory discussed in Chapter 2, quantitative techniques based on objective formal qualities must be viewed with a good deal of skepticism. As I have argued, an objectivist/formalist approach to landscape aesthetics is valid only within the realm of biologically based preferences. Only in that realm is it meaningful to consider the objective features of landscape in abstraction from the subject's experience of them. Outside that realm, cultural and personal values must also be considered and landscape aesthetics must be viewed in terms of the experiential interaction of the perceiver and the landscape. But since the experience of landscape is simultaneously biological, cultural and personal, it would rarely if ever be appropriate to consider only formal qualities in the evaluation of a landscape. Furthermore, if formal qualities are considered as such, then they must be qualities which symbolize a habitat conducive to human survival. If a formal quality cannot be justified by some type of habitat theory, then its inclusion in an evaluation model is suspect.

A related consideration involves the relationship between the aesthetic and the moral, practical and functional realms. I have argued that these realms are inextricably bound up together in the everyday experience of the landscape. As Kant observed, the aesthetic is the symbol of the moral or practical. And landscapes, by their very nature, are syntheses of the aesthetic and the functional. Thus landscape evaluation that ignores the necessary ties between aesthetics and these other realms is incomplete. This is simply another way of saying that content and meaning must be considered simultaneously with form and other objective qualities. Quantitative evaluation techniques often do not allow for the kind of assessment that goes beyond surface phenomena to include a critique of moral and functional values. Thus the results of quantitative analyses may be quite superficial and inadequate for the purposes of informing policy.

### The Shafer *et al.* Model

Criticism of this model (Shafer, Hamilton, and Schmidt, 1969; Shafer and Mietz, 1970; Shafer and Brush, 1977) may be considered by some to be beating a dead horse since it has been subjected to detailed attention elsewhere (*e.g.* Weinstein, 1976; Carlson, 1977). The model does, however, provide a gross example of the inadequacy of formalist approaches in quantitative landscape evaluation. The stated purpose of Shafer *et al.* was to develop a quantitative method for predicting the aesthetic preferences of landscape scenes, thereby providing a basis for making objective decisions regarding the use of natural scenic resources.

Their method involved the use of 100 black and white photographs of natural scenes in the United States. These scenes included mountains, meadows, forests and water, but not seascapes. Each of the photographs was divided into the following 'zones': (1) sky; (2) immediate vegetation; (3) intermediate vegetation; (4) distant vegetation; (5) immediate non-vegetation; (6) intermediate non-vegetation; (7) distant non-vegetation; (8) streams; (9) waterfalls; and (10) lakes. A ¼-inch grid overlay was used to obtain four types of measurements for each zone: (1) perimeter; (2) number of interior squares; (3) area; and (4) number of squares with vertical boundary edges. These measurements were taken directly from the surface of each photograph and did not attempt to assess the extent of each zone as it occurred on the ground. The researchers also identified six additional variables relating to the tonal quality of areas of sky, land and water. Altogether, 46 different variables were measured. The measurements of the numbers of interior squares and squares with vertical boundary edges were eliminated from further study because they were highly correlated with the measurements for area and per-imeter, respectively. This left 26 variables. Factor analysis and other considerations reduced the final set of variables to eight; however, the model estimated included the eight variables plus their squares and all possible multiplicative combinations of pairs of variables.

The researchers assessed preferences for the photographs in field tests conducted in state parks and recreation areas in the north-eastern and western United States. Interviews were conducted with randomly selected campers and 'day users', who ranked the photographs by preference. The resulting rank values were added and the total value for each photograph was designated as its preference score $(Y)$. By using multiple regression analysis, a mathematical equation was derived that included only those variables that jointly provided the best explanation of preference. The following appeared in the final model: perimeter of immediate vegetation $(X_1)$; perimeter of intermediate vegetation $(X_2)$; perimeter of distant vegetation $(X_3)$; area of intermediate vegetation $(X_4)$; area of any kind of water $(X_5)$; and area of distant non-vegetation $(X_6)$. The final estimated equation was as follows:

$$Y = 184.8 - 0.5436X_1 - 0.09298X_2 + 0.002069X_1X_3 + 0.0005538X_1X_4$$
$$- 0.002596X_3X_5 + 0.001634X_2X_6 - 0.008441X_4X_6 - 0.0004131X_4X_5$$
$$+ 0.0006666(X_1)^2 + 0.0001327(X_5)^2$$

This model explained 66 percent of the variation in the dependent variable $(Y)$. Thus the authors concluded that the model provides a useful means for quantifying aesthetic aspects of landscapes.

One immediately obvious problem with the Shafer *et al.* approach is that it was not informed by any theoretical considerations, except perhaps the implicit notion that formal characteristics of landscape photographs might be related to preferences. As I have argued, formal approaches to landscape aesthetics make sense only if one is focusing on the biological mode of aesthetic experience and the formal qualities one is measuring can be related explicitly to some form of habitat theory. But since Shafer *et al.* gave no attention to theory, their choice of variables is completely without justification. The variables do not even seem to make sense intuitively.

This kind of gross empiricism can often lead to spurious results. The methodology employed by Shafer *et al.* virtually guaranteed that the results would be spurious. Regression analysis simply measures linear relationships among variables; it does not identify cause and effect. Some kind of theory is required to causally link the independent variables (in this case, the formal characteristics of the landscape photographs) to the dependent variable (preference scores), before the results of regression analysis can be enlisted to support the theory. Lacking any kind of meaningful theories or hypotheses about the relationships between the dependent and independent variables, the results presented by Shafer *et al.* are highly suspect and impossible to interpret. Furthermore, the method of employing a large number of variables in the estimated model (including squares and multiplicative combinations of variables) almost ensures that some combination of statistically significant independent variables will be found to 'explain' a significant percentage of the variation in the dependent variable. As Weinstein (1976) put it: 'With enough independent variables a regression equation can be derived that will correlate perfectly with *any* dependent variable, no matter how meaningless and inappropriate the predictors actually are' (p. 613). Thus the so-called 'objective' results of Shafer *et al.* are probably quite spurious. Shafer and Tooby's (1973) attempt to replicate the original study with results for Scottish respondents merely reported a high correlation between the two sets of preference scores and does not in any way justify the original specification of variables (Weinstein, 1976).

## The Scenic Beauty Estimation Model

This model (Daniel and Boster, 1976) was designed to assess aesthetic quality of forests and wildlands for management purposes. The authors maintained that quantitative evaluation methods can provide the means for taking into account intangibles such as aesthetic quality in the management of public lands such as forests. They argued that better land use decisions can be made if more objective data are available, including data about aesthetic quality. They also noted that there is little or no connection between designer or manager and the client or public in the case of the management of public lands. Quantitative assessment of public preferences can therefore help to bridge the gap between the manager and the public.

The Scenic Beauty Estimation (SBE) Model uses color slides of an area taken in accordance with a stratified random sampling procedure. These are shown to groups of observers ranging from the 'general public' to forest managers. Each observer independently judges the scenic beauty of the area represented by each color slide. These judgments are usually recorded in terms of a 10-point scale, where 1 indicates very low scenic beauty and 10 indicates very high. These raw responses are transformed into standardized scores which control for the fact that different observers will apply the 10-point scale differently. These standardized scores are referred to as 'Scenic Beauty Estimates'.

One application of the SBE Model involved an attempt to relate Scenic Beauty Estimates to objective qualities of forest landscapes (Daniel and Schroeder, 1979). This was intended to allow the Model to be used for predictive purposes. The objective features included in this analysis were chosen on the basis of an intuitive sense that they had some bearing on aesthetic quality. Features such as 'openness' and 'average tree size' were considered. A panel of five judges rated 30 scenes for each of the objective features using a six-point scale. For example, the scale for openness ranged from 1 (very closed in, can't see very far) to 6 (very open, almost unlimited views). Scenic Beauty Estimates were then correlated with the ratings of objective features. Among other things, it was found that the amount of downed wood was negatively correlated with scenic beauty and that openness and tree size were positively correlated with each other and with scenic beauty.

A later study used more systematic methods for assessing the objective features of forests in the Coconino National Forest, Arizona. In this study, regression analysis was used to relate Scenic Beauty Estimates and objective landscape features in a Scenic Beauty Prediction Model. Factors such as man-caused downed wood (slash) and small trees were negatively related to scenic beauty whereas large trees and the amount of ground covers such as grass were positively related to scenic beauty. The authors emphasized that any predictions made using the Model would probably be valid only for forest landscapes similar to those used in developing the Model.

The SBE Model avoids several of the conceptual problems evident in the Shafer *et al.* model. For example, the concept of landscape aesthetics underlying the SBE Model explicitly avoids the problems of formalism and objectivism. In particular, the designers of the Model emphasized the 'interactive' nature of aesthetic experience and the implications of that for aesthetic quality: 'scenic beauty is inferred from a judgment made by a human observer in response to his perception of a landscape' (p. 13). They were quite aware of the importance of cultural symbolism and compared Scenic Beauty Estimates for 26 different groups representing a variety of interests. They noted, for example, that 'range interests' (those with a primary interest in raising cattle) preferred more open, grassy landscapes, and that landscape architects were generally more critical than other groups, having lower overall ratings for the various landscapes included in the study.

The authors also recognized the difficulties involved in using public preferences as a guide to forest management:

Assessment of the preferences of the 'general public' presents many problems. An undifferentiated 'average' of public opinion may not be a useful or meaningful guide to land management policy. It would imply that all public preferences should be weighted equally, and ignores the fact that particular actions in certain areas may have a great deal of impact on one segment of society, but have very little (or even the opposite) effect on other segments. (Daniel and Boster, 1976, p. 37)

The authors also mentioned that some landscape management decisions must remain 'subjective', apparently allowing room for creativity on the part of the manager. This could, however, have been addressed more explicitly in the Model, as Daniel and Boster were not specific as to how Scenic Beauty Estimates should be taken into account by decision makers.

Some of the habitat theory discussed in Chapter 4 might be helpful in specifying the variables to be included in the predictive model. The authors' approach to specifying the model was to start with a fairly extensive list of variables that were related intuitively to aesthetic quality. They initially used stepwise regression analysis to attempt to determine the most important variables. They noted, however, that some of the variables (such as tree size and openness) were correlated with each other and that regression analysis is unable to assign significance properly when explanatory variables are not truly independent. This meant that judgment had to be used in making the final decisions as to which variables should be included in the model. Both the initial and the final decisions about variables to be included in the model could have benefited from the ideas of prospect-refuge theory and information-processing theory.

Finally, the predictive model could have benefited from a more explicit treatment of cultural values. For example, it was found that downed wood had a negative relationship with aesthetic quality, but that man-caused slash had a more significant negative effect than naturally downed wood. Whereas the general negative effect of downed wood could be explained by aspects of prospect-refuge theory (locomotion is impeded) and information-processing theory (legibility is reduced), the differential significance of man-caused slash must be explained by cultural symbolism. For this reason, slash may be evaluated differently by different groups. Environmentalists might view slash as an example of man's irresponsible use of natural resources, while individuals involved in the wood products industry might view things quite differently.

**An Assessment Procedure for Countryside Landscapes**

The Assessment Procedure for Countryside Landscapes was developed for the US Soil Conservation Service (Schauman and Pfender, 1982; Schauman, 1988a) and was subsequently applied in an evaluation of scenic corridors in Whatcom County, Washington (Auld and Porter, 1984; Schauman, 1988b) and extended with another case

**Table 6**   Indicators of scenic quality used in the Assessment Procedure for Countryside Landscapes

---

*As a basis for technical judgment:*
1. Character – A range of landscape conditions from a visually congruent assembly of landscape elements to an incongruent assembly of landscape elements as judged by the visual criteria of form, color, texture and scale/proportion.
2. Uniqueness – A range of landscape conditions from rare to ordinary, or landscape elements as measured by relative quantity and distribution.
3. Fragility – A range of landscape conditions from a high capacity to absorb change (additions or deletions) without diminishing the visual environment of either the existing landscape or of the additions, to an inability of the landscape to contain any additions as measured by designated visual absorption factors.
4. Fitness – A range of landscape conditions from those connoting an appearance of care, tidiness, stewardship, or conservation to those exhibiting a distinct lack thereof, such as derelict, unkempt, littered, eroding or battered landscapes.
5. Structure – A range of landscape spatial conditions from those areas offering unlimited but undefined views to those areas offering no vista or where all views are blocked.
6. Information – A range of landscape conditions from those that provide maximum information to those in which all of the parts may be visible at first glance, contain no interest or little information or contain disordered information (chaotic).

*As a basis for public input:*
7. Preference – A range from 'like very much' to 'dislike'.
8. Meaning – A range of opinions about the value of the landscape defined by individual interpretations, social contacts and time relationships.

---

Source: Schauman and Pfender, 1982, pp. 10–11.

study of Whatcom County (Porter, 1987). This evaluation method applies to 'countryside' landscapes in order to focus on those landscapes that are neither urban nor wilderness. This includes primarily agricultural landscapes, but also other types of scenes often found in agricultural areas.

The first part of the procedure involves a landscape classification system which includes a hierarchy of scales - national, regional, local and site. At the highest level, the system includes land use categories such as cultivated lands, orchards, grazable lands and so forth, which emphasize the visual characteristics of countryside landscapes. The significance of this classification system is unclear, however, since it did not seem to play a role of any sort in the subsequent evaluation of specific landscapes. The authors did note that the 'evaluation indicators' could be applied at any of the four levels of the classification system's hierarchy. However, the subsequent application to Whatcom County (Auld and Porter, 1984) used a system of 'landscape units' unrelated to the classification system. Many of the landscape units referred to landscapes unique to Whatcom County and, furthermore, the landscape units did not seem to have been applied in any way in the evaluation of scenic corridors in the County. Since the classification system seems to be largely irrelevant, it will not be mentioned in the following discussion.

The core of the procedure is a set of 'evaluation indicators', which provide a framework for technical judgments by landscape experts as well as input from the public. The indicators are listed in Table 6. All or only some of the indicators may be used in any particular evaluation process, although the authors recommend that each process include a combination of both technical judgment and public input. The primary questions to be addressed in the following paragraphs concern the theoretical basis for an evaluation process based on this set of indicators. It should be noted that Schauman and Pfender admitted that 'The question of choice and validity of evaluation indicators is no small problem' (p. 105).

The authors of the procedure gave a significant amount of attention to theory, even going so far as to suggest a tripartite paradigm: 'Our attitudes toward the countryside landscape are culturally biased and are a result of our collective evolution as a human species and our experience as individuals' (Schauman and Pfender, 1982, p. 23). They followed that statement with a review of some general cultural attitudes towards countryside landscapes, which they labeled 'agrarianism', 'ruralism' and 'pastoralism'. They also noted that cultural values differ from place to place and change over time and that the values of the public may differ from those of the experts. For this reason, public input is needed to guide professional decision makers. Professionals, however, have specific insights that can serve as a basis for 'technical' judgments. Some of these insights are based on intuitive criteria used widely by design professionals, including formal factors such as 'form, line, color, and texture'. Schauman and Pfender also considered biological bases for aesthetics - particularly the concepts of Appleton and the Kaplans - under the rubric 'emotional responses'. No specific attention was given to the role of individual experience.

Some problems with the indicators chosen by Schauman and Pfender include the reference to formal qualities in the technical criterion 'Character', which refers to what could be called harmony or congruency. It should go without saying at this point that judgments regarding congruency or incongruency depend upon cultural significances and values and not just superficial formal qualities.

Thus, the reference to 'form, color, texture, and scale/proportion' is inadequate. This is not to say that Character would be an inappropriate criterion if redefined, since it seems to be closely related to the concept of good fit, which was Alexander's criterion of good design. Two of the remaining criteria also deal with good fit – 'Fragility' and 'Fitness' – and perhaps the relationships among these criteria need to be reconsidered.

Furthermore, it is evident that 'Meaning' is manifested in each of the three criteria related to good fit and cannot be treated in isolation. The subsequent application of the procedure by Auld and Porter (1984), which did not use the indicator Meaning, nevertheless produced some results that can be interpreted only by reference to cultural values. In her later study of Whatcom County, Porter (1987) found, among other things, that local farmers preferred spatially defined scenes with farm buildings to spatially defined 'natural' scenes, contradicting the findings of Ulrich and others who have concluded that humans prefer natural landscapes to those with buildings. Porter observed: 'The special meaning of the agricultural symbols of the countryside for the farming population upsets the preference pattern seen in other studies of common nature' (p. 67). The general implication for the procedure is that cultural values need to be addressed more carefully.

Another problem concerns the 'Structure' and 'Information' criteria, which reflect a rather incomplete or clumsy translation of theory into practice. Structure addresses the prospect part of Appleton's theory, but neglects refuge. Information attempts to grasp something of the Kaplans' information-processing theory, but it does not address explicitly the distinct elements of that theory (see Chapter 4). Instead, it refers to a range from maximum information to no information or disordered information, which actually seems to be two ranges since no information and disordered information are hardly the same thing.

Although the procedure gives an important role to landscape experts, it restricts that role to the making of 'technical' judgments based on established criteria. The procedure thus fails to allow an opportunity for innovative strategies to play a role in landscape evaluation. Another problem with the procedure is that it does not specify which of the indicators should be used in any given situation, leaving that to an *ad hoc* decision on the part of the evaluators. While the authors maintain that this is necessary to allow evaluators to adapt the procedure to the circumstances of each problem, it seems to stem more from uncertainty about the validity of the indicators.

## Landscape Criticism as a Model for Landscape Evaluation

Carlson (1977) provides a very useful critique of several of the assumptions underlying quantitative evaluation techniques. Among other things, he questions the equation of scenic quality with public landscape preferences. Basing landscape design and management decisions on public preferences 'may have the effects of standardizing current aesthetic approaches to the environment and inhibiting the growth of new and better approaches' (p. 147). Carlson noted a need to pay attention to subtle qualities in the landscape as well as the more obvious appeal of scenes such as those containing mountains or waterfalls. Thus models based on public preferences predict the 'lowest common denominator', or landscape types with the most obvious public appeal.

Carlson also observed that, in other domains, such as art or literature, the evaluation of aesthetic quality is the prerogative of experts, such as art or literary critics. He argued that it would be absurd to use a public opinion poll as the basis for decisions on works to be included in an art gallery, for example. By analogy, he urged that the best judges of scenic quality would be 'environmental critics'. Such individuals would have a combination of sensibility toward aesthetic qualities and knowledge about landscape processes. The main reason society does not rely on landscape critics for landscape evaluation is that we have not yet fully developed a role for such individuals in our society.

While Carlson's analogy with art criticism provides an important insight, it is not entirely apt. There is a significant difference between works of art, such as paintings or novels, and landscapes. As I pointed out in Chapter 1, landscapes are inescapably public. Unlike most works of art, landscapes must be encountered by the public. It therefore follows that public preferences should have a greater part to play in evaluating the aesthetic quality of a landscape than in, say, evaluating the aesthetic quality of a painting. Thus I believe Carlson goes too far in characterizing public preferences as lowest common denominators. Assessments of public preferences – including quantitative measurements – can be an important source of information for landscape experts. In particular, such assessments can give experts an indication of the values of the groups that experience a landscape. This information can illustrate differences among the values of the different groups that make up the public, as well as differences between the views of the general public and those of the experts.

Nevertheless, Carlson is correct in warning against the stultifying effects of relying solely upon public preferences as a guide for design and management decisions. Here Carlson is concerned to allow for what I have termed creative or innovative personal strategies. The qualities required of the environmental critic - sensibility and knowledge - are very much like the qualities that define the creative person (see Chapter 6). The creative individual has both an in-depth understanding of landscape processes and a sensibility that allows him to see in unconventional ways. I would characterize such a person as a 'landscape critic' rather than an 'environmental critic', for the same reasons I prefer 'landscape' over 'environmental' aesthetics (see Chapter 1). Similarly, I prefer the term landscape criticism to environmental criticism.

Carlson is correct to emphasize the role of the expert in landscape evaluation (*cf.* Carlson, 1990). The results of public preference surveys should inform, rather than dictate, the decisions made by experts. Public preferences are only one element of the context that must be considered in all its various dimensions in the design and management of landscapes. Thus I offer 'landscape criticism' as a model of landscape evaluation. Landscape criticism is not a new concept; geographers, for example, have already attempted to appropriate it (Lewis, 1973). And Sancar (1989) has argued that architectural criticism should be expanded to embrace the entire landscape. This is remarkably consistent with my observation in Chapter 1 that the appropriate aesthetic object in architecture is landscape. Indeed, the best architectural critics have always been concerned with issues that go beyond the design of individual buildings. One of the most promising trends in architectural criticism (and design) today - 'critical regionalism' - is a model for landscape criticism. The following chapter explores the concept of critical regionalism as a facet of postmodernism. I shall argue that critical regionalism offers an approach to landscape criticism and design that is quite consistent with the aesthetic theory developed in the first six chapters of this book.

# CHAPTER 8
# POSTMODERNISM

One of the most prominent issues today in the fields of architecture, landscape architecture, urban design and related fields concerns the nature and import of postmodernism. It is therefore of interest to consider whether the aesthetic theory presented in this book has anything to say about it. Postmodernism has many different definitions and has been discussed by theorists in a number of disciplines from numerous points of view. Much of this chapter will be devoted to sketching out some of the salient ideas about the phenomenon of postmodernism. First, I shall define postmodernism by contrasting it with modernism. Secondly, I shall compare two different types of postmodernism and advocate what has been called 'critical regionalism'. This will be followed by a consideration of the implications of the political-economic conditions of postmodernity for critical regionalism. Finally, the chapter is concluded by applying the aesthetic theory developed in Chapters 1 to 6 to the postmodern debate.

## Modernism and Postmodernism

As the term suggests, *postmodernism* is characterized by the ways in which it is different from modernism. In its most general sense, postmodernism refers to a rejection of the rationalism of the *Enlightenment*, as embraced by modernism. Modernism adopted wholeheartedly the Enlightenment idea that rationality could be applied to solve social problems and that mankind's condition could thereby be progressively improved toward some unitary, consensual end. As Habermas (1985) noted, nineteenth-century romanticism led to another theme of twentieth-century modernity; this was the novel idea that modernity did not involve idealization and imitation of some past era. Thus modernism came to reject tradition and it 'freed itself from all specific historical ties' (p. 4). A related influence of romanticism was an emphasis on the artist's originality and creativity.

In architecture, modernism came to be associated with a specific aesthetic style, known as *functionalism*. Functionalism was a clear extension of modernism's rationalism and abandonment of tradition. It involved a rejection of all historical references and an emphasis on a machine aesthetics that expressed an image of rationality. Ornament was not permitted unless it contributed to the aesthetics of the machine. As Mumford (1962) noted, functionalism 'sought to make the new buildings *look* as if they respected the machine, no matter what the materials or methods of construction' (p. 77). Functionalism was an 'International Style' that was appropriate universally, at all places and times, regardless of the cultural, historical, climatological or topographical context. Modernism also comprised the idea that each building should be a strong statement of the architect's creative ability.

In urban planning, modernism was epitomized by the idea that it would be possible to resolve urban problems through a rational process of comprehensive city planning. Land use could be rationalized through zoning, which would insure the separation of incompatible land uses and prevent congestion by enforcing low densities. Slums, and their attendant social problems, could be excised through urban renewal. More radical thinkers such as Le Corbusier diagnosed the city's problems and found that major surgery was needed to combat the evils of congestion and slums. Le Corbusier's *La ville radieuse* (1964) required a complete abandonment of the historic fabric of the city, including the 'death of the street', in favor of a 'dictatorial' plan.

The failures of modernism in architecture and planning are well-known (see *e.g.* Brolin, 1976; Blake, 1977; Wolfe, 1981). Generally, it is argued that, instead of improving the human condition, modernism has contributed to its impoverishment. More specifically, and perhaps unfairly, modernism has been blamed for the destruction of the city. Prince Charles, one of the most prominent critics of modernism, contributed to the fray by criticizing modern architects and planners for destroying London. Comparing them to the German Luftwaffe, he said (quoted by Lohr, 1987): 'You have to give this much to the Luftwaffe – when it knocked down our buildings, it didn't replace them with anything more offensive than rubble. We did that.' As has already been suggested, however, the most fundamental critique of modernism is with respect to its uncritical acceptance of Enlightenment rationalism. The rationality of modernism is viewed skeptically as a naive optimism; there is no longer any faith in the idea of progress. As Huxtable (1980) put it: 'Today there is no certainty about anything anymore. There are no longer any approved verities to hang onto, no yardsticks or ideals that safely and universally apply' (p. 22).

Huyssen (1981), Lyotard (1984) and others have contributed to the general critique of modernism, while Habermas is an important defender. Both Huyssen and Lyotard emphasize the value of pluralism, while Habermas emphasizes consensus. Huyssen, for example, wrote:

> Habermas ignores the fact that the very idea of a wholistic modernity and of a totalizing view of history has become anathema in the 1970s . . . The critical deconstruction of enlightenment rationalism and logocentrism by theoreticians of culture, the decentering of traditional notions of identity, the fight of women and gays for a legitimate social and sexual identity outside of the parameters of male, heterosexual vision, the search for alternatives in our relationship with nature, including the nature of our own bodies – all these phenomena, which are key to the culture of the 1970s, make Habermas' proposition to complete the project of modernity questionable, if not undesirable. (p. 38)

In this same vein, planners are no longer enamored of grand comprehensive schemes; they are more comfortable with incrementalism and muddling-through. The modern emphasis on the use of zoning to rationalize city form by separating supposedly incompatible uses and maintaining low densities seems simplistic and contrary to what makes for an interesting and lively urban setting (Jacobs, 1961). Along with Robert Venturi (1966), planners have come to appreciate 'messy vitality over obvious unity' (p. 22). The emphasis on clearance of slums and other problematic parts of the city is viewed as being crudely insensitive to the value of existing social networks and historic forms.

Architects have come to design buildings that respect the various dimensions of their contexts; it is no longer desirable for each building to be a distinct creative statement that stands out from its environment. Brolin (1980) maintained that the modernists' 'indifference – indeed hostility – to harmonious continuity comes from the modernists' violent denunciation of derivative architectural forms' (p. 7). Today, an eclectic permissiveness prevails with respect to historic form and ornament. Architects now appreciate the symbolic function of architecture and the symbolism of historic forms and ornamentation. In adopting the narrow functionalism of the aesthetics of the machine, architects had denied the importance of symbolism: 'In properly rejecting antiquated symbols, they . . . also rejected human needs, interests, sentiments, values, that must be given full play in every complete structure' (Mumford, 1952, p. 86).

This overview, however brief, has catalogued some of the fundamental differences between modernism and postmodernism. Modernism encompasses Enlightenment rationalism, denial of tradition, a universal functionalist style, prohibition of ornament and symbolism, a romantic individualism which valued buildings that stand out rather than fit in, and a penchant for grand, totalitarian solutions to urban problems. Postmodernism, by contrast, is characterized by skeptical distrust of human rational abilities, respect for tradition, an eclectic aesthetic, recognition of the importance of ornament and symbol, a contextualism that values buildings that attend to their surroundings, and an incremental approach to the solution of urban problems (*cf.* Stern, 1977). While this contrast of modernism and postmodernism has contributed to the purpose of defining, or at least describing, the latter, it is inadequate because it masks a major split within postmodernism. As Foster (1985) observed, there are really two distinct types of postmodernism: 'a postmodernism of resistance and a postmodernism of reaction' (p. xii). The critical dialogue about these two types constitutes the postmodern debate.

## The Postmodern Debate

According to Foster (1985): 'In cultural politics today, a basic opposition exists between a postmodernism which seeks to deconstruct modernism and resist the status quo and a postmodernism which repudiates the former to celebrate the latter' (pp. xi-xii). These two streams of postmodernism are clearly evident in architecture and planning. The postmodernism of resistance is advocated by writers such as Boyer (1986), Frampton (1982, 1985), Huxtable (1980) and Jencks (1978), while the postmodernism of reaction is clearly exemplified in the work of Venturi (1966) and Venturi, Scott Brown and Izenour (1977).

In architecture, the postmodernism of reaction is strictly a matter of style, in the narrow, mannerist sense of the word. Venturi (1966) spurred a radical change in the reigning tastes of the modern movement when he rejected the exclusionary style of functionalism in favor of a relatively eclectic, but purely formal, contextualism. Historical allusion and ornament became desirable elements of architecture and it was no longer necessary for buildings to express the functionalist image of rationalism. The eclecticism of Venturi, Scott Brown and Izenour (1977) even went so far as to extol the 'commercial vernacular' of the Las Vegas strip. But again this was strictly a formal conceit, devoid of any critical consideration of content. This kind of postmodernism has been rightfully criticized

as 'an instrumental pastiche of pop- or pseudo-historical forms'
(Foster, 1985, p. xii), 'do-it-yourself history' (Huxtable, 1980, p. 26),
'cardboard scenography' (Frampton, 1982, p. 76), or an example of
'precisely that avalanche of academicism, commercialism, and
kitsch that is always ready to swamp our culture in the absence of
a tradition vigorous enough to resist it' (Kramer, 1987, p. 327).
Huxtable (1980) summed up the problem: 'It takes a creative act, not
clever cannibalism, to turn a building into art' (p. 26). More recently,
Goldberger (1987) noted that some current architecture students are
so dissatisfied with the superficiality of prevalent postmodern theory
and practice that they are reverting to modernist forms: 'they fear
that postmodernism is unable to look at architecture as something
deeper than a question of choosing a few pretty cornices for a few
multimillion-dollar houses' (p. 56).

A reactionary postmodernism in planning parallels that in architecture (Dear, 1986). Boyer (1986) and Jacobs and Appleyard (1987)
noted an inability to plan the form of the city on the part of contemporary planners: an abdication to market forces of control over urban
form. Those authors, together with Krumholz (1987), also lamented
planners' apparent lack of social ideals. Instead of a reformist
concern with improving the quality of life in the city, there is
passive accommodation of the market. Planning is a matter of
managing programs and reacting to market demands rather than a
matter of imagining the future of the city (Neutze, 1988).

In contrast to the postmodernism of reaction is the critical postmodernism of resistance. According to Cooper (quoted by Ganem,
1987): 'As soon as we get through all this nonsense about fake
Greek, fake Roman, fake whatever, the serious practitioners will be
doing things that reflect very positively the place where they're
being built' (p. 70). And: 'If there is a trend that does make sense
right now, it is a very powerful sense of regionalism.' Frampton
(1985) called this trend *critical regionalism*, a term he attributed to
Tzonis and Lefaivre (1981; *cf.* Fuller, 1986, who proposed an
'informed provincialism'). Frampton, more than anyone else, has
succeeded in elucidating a meaningful direction for postmodernism.
Critical regionalism is a highly self-critical approach to architecture
and planning. It recognizes the importance of context, but this
recognition is not limited to the acknowledgement of existing
architectural forms. It also appreciates the significance of local
culture, social institutions, political issues, building techniques,
climate, topography and other elements of the regional context. The
critical regionalist is aware of universal techniques but does not try
to apply them arbitrarily, without respect to local conditions. At the
same time, the critical regionalist does not resort to a sentimental

**Plate 29**   Two postmodern buildings

vernacular or a reactionary historicizing.

Plate 29 illustrates some of the differences between the post-modernism of resistance, or critical regionalism, and reactionary postmodernism, particularly the matter of attention to local architectural styles. Robert Stern's building (at left) reflects a careful study of its surroundings, while Philip Johnson and John Burgee's tower (immediately to the right of Stern's building) is an arbitrary assemblage of historical forms. As Goldberger (1988) observed: 'it is hard not to feel that if the designers in Mr Johnson and Mr Burgee's office were looking at books for inspiration, Mr Stern and his colleagues were wearing out shoe leather on the streets of Back Bay' (p. 31).

The critical regionalist goes beyond the vernacular and the universal in a creative synthesis which seeks to increase *the cultural density of the built fabric*' (Frampton, 1982, p. 76). This is another way of saying that the critical regionalist seeks to enhance the identities of places, to intensify their cultural significance. Webber's (1964) 'non-place urban realm' is explicitly rejected as a model for city form (Frampton, 1985). The critical regionalist realizes that urban form must be bounded and defined if it is to serve as a repository for human meaning. Critical regionalism's 'salient cultural precept is "place" creation; its general model is the "enclave" – that is, the bounded urban fragment against which the inundation of the place-less, consumerist environment will find itself momentarily checked' (Frampton, 1982, p. 81).

## Political-Economic Conditions of Postmodernity

Writers such as Harvey (1987, 1989) and Albertsen (1988) have linked postmodern design with a broad transformation of capitalist political economy dating from the early 1970s. Stated very simply, a relatively rigid 'Fordist' mode of standardized mass production has been replaced by a régime of 'flexible accumulation' characterized by considerable fluidity of both production processes and consumption patterns. This transformation is aided by the globalization of capital and financial markets. Global capital and flexible accumulation are simultaneously creative and destructive. As they create new patterns of production and consumption, they also destroy old patterns. A plant closing may destroy a town or the gentrification of a neighborhood may displace low-income residents. According to Harvey, an understanding of the processes of flexible accumulation leads one to be skeptical about the potential of critical regionalism and similar models of the postmodernism of resistance.

The link between the post-Fordist political-economic régime and postmodern aesthetics is in the realm of the production of 'symbolic capital'. To an increasing extent, producers attempt to stimulate consumption by production of highly differentiated products that symbolize the tastes and social status of the consumer. Commodities, including urban neighborhoods, have become 'aestheticized' to the point that they are consumed to a large extent for symbolic purposes. For Harvey, aesthetics refers to what are essentially superficial, formal qualities devoid of any moral content (cf. Cosgrove, 1990). Indeed, in *The condition of postmodernity* (1989), Harvey explicitly followed the main thrust of Kant's aesthetic philosophy, with its perverse separation of the aesthetic and the moral realms. For Harvey, the postmodern emphasis on creation of differentiated places is potentially dangerous precisely because it is aesthetic (in the narrow Kantian sense). As an example of this he gives the extreme aestheticization of German culture under the Nazis. Harvey also reminds us that many of those theorists who emphasize place creation are followers of Heidegger, who supported the Nazi régime. In Heidegger's thought, aesthetics is associated with a state of *being* whereas what is needed to resist or – even better – transform the existing political-economic régime is a critical or even revolutionary process of *becoming*.

It must be admitted that the example of the Nazis is an extreme case. It is also a case of what we might call 'uncritical aestheticization' rather than 'aestheticization' *per se*. As I argued in Chapter 2, aesthetic decisions are necessarily also practical or moral ones. Without the practical or moral dimension, the formal aspects of aesthetics lose their meaning. Thus Frampton advocates 'critical regionalism' rather than mere 'regionalism'. The latter would correspond to an approach to design and planning that would be aesthetic only in the narrow Kantian sense. The former, however, goes far beyond the limitations of Kant's aesthetics. As I have shown, even Kant himself was ultimately forced to admit that the aesthetic is the symbol of the moral.

But Harvey does not find much cause for celebration in Frampton's critical regionalism. The ineluctable forces of global capital are too powerful, according to Harvey, to be resisted significantly by local or regional efforts. The possibilities of movements such as critical regionalism are 'small beer compared to the "creative destruction" with which flexible accumulation typically scars the fabric of the city' (Harvey, 1987, p. 280). Albertsen, in contrast, is more optimistic, suggesting that locally based 'networks of power' may effectively resist global pressures.

Harvey's position with respect to critical regionalism may be in large part due to his Marxist point of view. It must be recognized that Marxism - like capitalism - is one of those grand modernist solutions to social problems eyed skeptically by the postmodernist. Neither the pure Marxist nor the pure capitalist can be satisfied with incremental, local solutions, since it is the entire political-economic system that must be overhauled. In contrast, the post-modernist (or, at least, the critical regionalist) realizes that perhaps the problem is not quite so total and perhaps its solution might be achieved through a series of small steps. The best solution to the problems of the existing political-economic régime may in fact be some kind of synthesis of capitalism and socialism. The means for achieving that solution may involve the incremental introduction of elements of one system into political economies dominated exces-sively by the other system. In any case, it seems that Harvey's diagnosis of the problem leads to a prescription for inactivity on the part of planners and designers, who might in his view be seen to be wasting their time pursuing feeble local solutions to inexorable global problems. Although critical regionalism will often entail a difficult struggle on the part of planners and designers, there seems to be cause for greater sanguinity than Harvey allows. As Kolb (1990) put it: 'We do not have to choose between architecture and revolution' (p. 162).

### Aesthetic Theory and Postmodernism

The theory of landscape aesthetics provides clear support for the postmodernism of resistance, critical regionalism. Although the implications of the theory are only rudimentary, critical regionalism is patently consistent with them. The theory of aesthetics presented in previous chapters is based primarily on the idea that human beings have three modes of existence deriving from three distinct developmental processes. The three processes were identified by Vygotsky as phylogenesis (or biological evolution), sociogenesis (or cultural history) and ontogenesis (or personal development). The three modes of existence corresponding to these developmental processes have been referred to as the *Umwelt*, *Mitwelt* and *Eigenwelt*, or the biological, cultural and personal worlds. These, in turn, correspond to three modes of aesthetic experience. While these three modes may manifest themselves as distinct phenomena in the experience of landscape (as, for example, in 'limbic intensive' experience) they have been used in this book primarily as an analytical framework that helps one to organize and understand the various components of landscape experience. The actual experience of landscape is some kind of synthesis of the three modes. As a consequence of this, it is quite difficult to determine in most instances precisely which aspects of landscape experience are biological, cultural or personal.

Theories about the biological basis for aesthetics are the most speculative of all and it is quite risky to attempt to make any applications given the severe limitations of current knowledge. I have argued, however, that biological theories of landscape aesthetics are necessarily forms of *habitat theory*, meaning that aesthetic preferences must be for landscapes which appear to enhance survival. This theory seems to explain why humans generally seem to prefer parklike scenery. Appleton's elaboration of habitat theory, which he calls *prospect-refuge theory*, seems to explain why humans like views and, particularly, views from protected, secure places. It also suggests an explanation for the thrill one experiences in moving from tightly enclosed spaces into much more open ones. The Kaplans' work on *information-processing theory* is another significant elaboration of habitat theory. They note that legibility and mystery are both particularly important. Legibility in the landscape is defined as those qualities that suggest one will be able to understand the landscape and orient oneself, whereas mystery implies that additional exploration could yield useful information. Generally, these findings about possible biological 'laws' do not really tell designers much more than they already understood intuitively. For example, Cullen's *Townscape* (1961) clearly reflects an understanding of the principles of prospect and refuge.

It is, however, possible to make some further, but rather tentative, connections between the biological theory of landscape aesthetics and critical regionalism. The critical regionalist's concern with the creation of meaningful places necessarily involves an emphasis on contained urban forms or enclaves and their boundaries. This emphasis seems to be quite compatible with the implications of Appleton's prospect-refuge theory. It is clearly impossible to have a dialectic of refuge and prospect or refuge and hazard without bounded, well-defined spaces. Some examples may help to explain what I mean.

Some of the most satisfying spaces are enclaves open to prospects. One thinks particularly of the Piazza San Marco in Venice. A less familiar example is in the French hill town of Cordes. Smith (1977) described the two squares in the center of Cordes: 'One is partly covered, in a manner which is common in France, with a kind of enlarged version of a medieval barn. This space is tightly enclosed except for one corner which provides access up a wide flight of steps to a higher plateau, shaded by tall trees and placed with a dramatic view over the distant hills' (p. 133). While these types of traditional urban spaces serve as ideals for the postmodernism of resistance, the postmodernism of reaction is not particularly concerned with the enclosure of exterior space. For example, Venturi, Scott Brown and Izenour (1977) were willing to place the A&P parking lot in the same historical tradition of 'vast space' as Versailles, despite the lack of enclosure of the former: 'The space that divides high-speed highway and low, sparse buildings produces no enclosure and little direction. To move through a piazza is to move between high enclosing forms. To move through this landscape [*i.e.* that of Las Vegas] is to move over vast expansive texture: the megatexture of the commercial landscape' (p. 13). In contrast, the critical regionalist would characterize the A&P parking lot and the Las Vegas landscape as 'anti-space' or 'lost space', to use the terms of Peterson (1980) or Trancik (1986).

With respect to the cultural mode of aesthetic experience, there are quite obvious points of tangency between aesthetic theory and the postmodernism of resistance. The cultural mode is addressed by Costonis' cultural stability-identity theory, which emphasizes the symbolic meanings of places for groups of people. Aesthetic value is attached to places that afford symbols of cultural stability and identity. Critical regionalism is similarly concerned with cultural stability and identity. The critical regionalist wants to intensify cultural identity by increasing the 'cultural density' of places. The reactionary postmodernist, on the other hand, seems to be preoccupied with formal conceits and to have little concern for the cultural significance of those forms.

The personal mode of aesthetic experience is also addressed by critical regionalism. I have identified the personal mode as the locus of creativity and the source of cultural change. Frampton (1982) agrees that creativity is essentially an individual matter: 'Regionalism . . . is not so much a collective effort as it is the output of a talented individual working with profound commitment to a particular local culture' (p. 81). I have also argued that a necessary condition for creativity is a thorough knowledge of the context of the problem to be solved. This is emphasized by the critical regionalist, who recognizes the fact that designing and planning necessarily occur within a context and inadequate attention to that context explains the failure of many design efforts. An excellent example of this is provided in Weirick's (1989) critique of Australia's new Parliament House. Weirick's paper may be viewed as a model of the critical regionalist's approach to design.

The design competition for the new Parliament House was opened in 1979 and the winners were announced in 1980. The winning design team was headed by the American architect Romaldo Giurgola. In a 1986 lecture, Giurgola (1987) attempted to portray his design for the Parliament House as one that was sensitive to its natural as well as cultural context. In regard to the natural context, he wrote:

Rather than being an imposition on the site, the Parliament building is generated by the natural state of the land configuration, just as democratic government is not an imposition on the community but rather originates organically from within the populace. As a consequence, the entire Parliament site is physically interconnected by means of internal green-space courtyards or linkages: starting from the walls of the two [legislative] Chambers and extending to the edges of the offices, to the peripheral park or eucalypt bosques, and ultimately to the city. (p. 45)

Speaking generally about the importance of the cultural context in design, Giurgola stated: 'I believe that it is in the making of coherent connections in time, history, and cultural identities ... that a building becomes true architecture. That making of clear connections with a cultural past and present is very different from the sophisticated playing with shapes which often passes for architecture today' (p. 44). These comments by Giurgola indicate an attitude that is, at least in principle, quite congruent with the concepts of critical regionalism. Weirick demonstrated very convincingly that the actual design for the new Parliament House unfortunately fails to meet the ideals of Giurgola's rhetoric. The building gives the appearance of being set into Canberra's Capital Hill, with two symmetrical curves of carefully maintained lawn extending over the central portion of the structure. In fact, the original hill and its vegetation (including some ancient native trees) were completely destroyed early in the construction process. Furthermore, the so-called 'Land Bridge' – a vast greensward connecting the forecourt of the new Parliament House to the old provisional Parliament House – required the obliteration of Camp Hill. It is hard to imagine how this vast rearrangement of the landscape and the introduction of non-native vegetation respect the natural conditions of the site. Indeed, as Weirick noted, Giurgola *had not even visited the site* when the design solution was conceived.

   Weirick made a number of penetrating observations about the relationship between the new Parliament House and its cultural context. Just as Giurgola's knowledge of the site was superficial, so was his knowledge of Australian culture. Weirick cited an unpublished lecture given by Giurgola in 1981 at Harvard's Graduate School of Design:

we only worked from a certain knowledge of Australia second-hand and mostly knowledge through books and publications and narratives and so forth. Of course the great Australian movies already were coming in this country so we could see the landscape at that point and also enjoy the wonderful stories depicted there which have tremendous importance, it seems to me, in the developing of the Australian culture ... I have been reading, of course, the short stories of Australia, Henry Lawson and Miles Franklin, the lady of *My Brilliant Career* and those are perhaps the best contact I can make ... with the country.

Seeing a few films and reading a few stories about a distant place hardly provide the depth of knowledge required for truly creative design. Unable to grasp Australian culture in any meaningful sense, the designers of the new Parliament House were reduced to decorating it primarily with symbols of the natural environment, such as the green marble columns in the foyer which evoke eucalypt trunks. As Weirick put it: 'Here in a big way, history has been transformed into nature. Social reality, the complexity of human acts, the contingency of history, the very presence of humanity - all eliminated' (p. 22). I have only touched upon Weirick's critique, but it should be clear that the new Parliament House represents a rather feeble attempt to respond to the problems of designing the symbol of a nation and placing a very large building on a difficult site. Admittedly, those problems were extraordinarily challenging ones. But the architect's response to those challenging problems was clearly inadequate.

In summary, the theory of landscape aesthetics provides a basis for embracing the postmodernism of resistance, critical regionalism, and rejecting the postmodernism of reaction. While the witty or ironic forms of reactionary postmodernism may be amusing to the architecturally erudite or appeasing to the general public, they ultimately reflect a superficial formalism or a passive commercialism. In planning, the acceptance of the status quo may satisfy market demands, but it fails to provide a vision of what the city could be. While the postmodernism of reaction may not be 'culturally disintegrative', it is surely culturally stultifying. As an alternative course for postmodernism, critical regionalism offers a means for achieving 'culturally vitalizing' change. Will postmodernism be defined by a creative and critical engagement with the various dimensions of local context? Or will it degenerate into triviality? If we are motivated to struggle against the latter trend, then postmodernism has the potential to be a powerfully invigorating force in the human landscape.

# BIBLIOGRAPHY

Albertsen, N., 1988, Postmodernism, post-Fordism, and critical social theory, in *Environment and Planning D: Society and Space*, **6** (3): 339-65.

Alexander, C., 1966, *Notes on the synthesis of form*, Harvard University Press, Cambridge, Mass.

Aoki, Y., 1983, An empirical study on the appraisals of landscape types by residential groups - Tsukuba Science City, in *Landscape Planning*, **10** (2): 109-30.

Apollinaire, G., 1949 [1913], *The cubist painters: aesthetic meditations*, trans. L. Abel, George Wittenborn, New York.

Appleton, J., 1975a, *The experience of landscape*, John Wiley and Sons, London.

Appleton, J., 1975b, Landscape evaluation: the theoretical vacuum, in *Transactions of the Institute of British Geographers*, **66**: 120-3.

Appleton, J., 1980, *Landscape in the arts and the sciences*, University of Hull, UK.

Appleton, J., 1984, Prospects and refuges re-visited, in *Landscape Journal*, **3** (2): 91-103.

Appleyard, D., 1969, City designers and the pluralistic city, in L. Rodwin, ed., *Planning urban growth and regional development: the experience of the Guayana program of Venezuela*, MIT Press, Cambridge, Mass.

Appleyard, D., 1979, The environment as a social symbol: within a theory of environmental action and perception, in *Journal of the American Planning Association*, **45** (2): 143-53.

Aristotle, 1968, *Aristotle's Poetics: a translation and commentary for students of literature*, trans. L. Golden, Prentice-Hall, Englewood Cliffs, N.J.

Arnheim, R., 1949, The Gestalt theory of expression, in *Psychological Review*, **56** (3): 156-71.

Arnheim, R., 1966, Order and complexity in landscape design, in *Toward a psychology of art: collected essays*, University of California Press, Berkeley.

Arnheim, R., 1977, *The dynamics of architectural form*, University of California Press, Berkeley.

Auld, M., Porter, M., 1984, *An assessment procedure for countryside landscapes: field test, Whatcom County, WA*, Soil Conservation Service Regional Office, Portland, Ore.

Bachelard, G., 1969, *The poetics of space*, trans. M. Jolas, Beacon Press, Boston.

Bachelard, G., 1970, Les nymphéas ou les surprises d'une aube d'été, in *Le droit de rêver*, Presses Universitaires de France, Paris.

Balling, J.D., Falk, J.H., 1982, Development of visual preference for natural environments, in *Environment and Behavior*, **14** (1): 5-28.

Barnett, H.G., 1953, *Innovation: the basis of cultural change*, McGraw-Hill, New York.

Barron, F., 1969, *Creative person and creative process*, Holt, Rinehart and Winston, New York.

Barzun, J., 1989, The paradoxes of creativity, in *The American Scholar*, **58** (Summer): 337-51.

Basch, D., 1972, The uses of aesthetics in planning: a critical review, in *Journal of Aesthetic Education*, **6** (3): 39-55.

Beardsley, M., 1966, *Aesthetics from classical Greece to the present: a short history*, Macmillan, New York.

Beardsley, M., 1982a, Aesthetic experience, in M.J. Wreen and D.M. Callen, eds., *The aesthetic point of view: selected essays*, Cornell University Press, Ithaca, NY.

Beardsley, M., 1982b, The aesthetic point of view, in M.J. Wreen and D.M. Callen, eds., *The aesthetic point of view: selected essays*, Cornell University Press, Ithaca, NY.

Beardsley, M., 1982c, The discrimination of aesthetic enjoyment, in M.J. Wreen and D.M. Callen, eds., *The aesthetic point of view: selected essays*, Cornell University Press, Ithaca, NY.

Bell, C., 1913, *Art*, Chatto and Windus, London.

Bergman, E.F., 1978, Review of *The experience of landscape*, by Jay Appleton, in *Geographical Review*, **68** (1): 106-8.

Berleant, A., 1982, The viewer in the landscape, in P. Bart, A. Chen and G. Francescato, eds., *EDRA 13: knowledge for design*, Environmental Design Research Association, College Park, Md.

Berleant, A., 1984, Aesthetic participation and the urban environment, in *Urban Resources*, **1** (1): 37-41.

Berleant, A., 1985, Toward a phenomenological aesthetics of environment, in D. Ihde and H.J. Silverman, eds., *Descriptions: selected studies in phenomenology and existential philosophy*, State University of New York Press, Albany.

Birnbaum, M.H., 1981, Thinking and feeling: a skeptical review, in *American Psychologist*, **36** (1): 99-101.

Blake, P., 1977, *Form follows fiasco: why modern architecture hasn't worked*, Little, Brown, Boston.

Bonyhady, T., 1985, *Images in opposition: Australian landscape painting 1801-1890*, Oxford University Press, Melbourne.

Bonyhady, T., 1987, *The colonial image: Australian painting 1800-1880*, Ellsyd Press/Australian National Gallery, Chippendale, NSW.

Bourassa, S.C., 1988, Toward a theory of landscape aesthetics, in *Landscape and Urban Planning*, **15** (3/4): 241-52.

Bourassa, S.C., 1989, Postmodernism in architecture and planning: what kind of style? in *Journal of Architectural and Planning Research*, **6** (4): 289-304.

Bourassa, S.C., 1990, A paradigm for landscape aesthetics, in *Environment and Behavior*, **22** (6): 787-812.

Boyer, M.C., 1986, The tragedy of city planning, in *CRIT*, **17** (Fall): 41-8.

Brolin, B.C., 1976, *The failure of modern architecture*, Van Nostrand Reinhold, New York.

Brolin, B.C., 1980, *Architecture in context: fitting new buildings with old*, Van Nostrand Reinhold, New York.

Buhyoff, G.J., Leuschner, W.A., Wellman, J.D., 1979, Aesthetic impacts of southern pine beetle damage, in *Journal of Environmental Management*, **8** (3): 261-7.

Buhyoff, G.J., Wellman, J.D., Harvey, H., Fraser, R.A., 1978, Landscape architects' interpretations of people's landscape preferences, in *Journal of Environmental Management*, **6** (3): 255-62.

Buhyoff, G.J., Wellman, J.D., Koch, N.E., Gauthier, L., Hultman, S., 1983, Landscape preference metrics: an international replication, in *Journal of Environmental Management*, **16** (2): 181-90.

Bullough, E., 1912, 'Psychical distance' as a factor in art and as an aesthetic principle, in *British Journal of Psychology*, **5** (2): 87-98.

Bunkśe, E.V., 1977, Review of *The experience of landscape*, by Jay Appleton, in *Annals of the Association of American Geographers*, **67** (1): 149-51.

Bunkśe, E.V., 1978, Commoner attitudes toward landscape and nature, in *Annals of the Association of American Geographers*, **68** (4): 551-66.

Bunkśe, E.V., 1981, Humboldt and an aesthetic tradition in geography, in *Geographical Review*, **71** (2): 127-46.

Burke, E., 1958 [1757], *A philosophical enquiry into the origin of our ideas of the sublime and beautiful*, J.T. Boulton, ed., Routledge and Kegan Paul, London.

Butzer, K.W., 1977, Environment, culture, and human evolution, in *American Scientist*, **65** (5): 572-84.

Carlson, A., 1977, On the possibility of quantifying scenic beauty, in *Landscape Planning*, **4** (2): 131-72.

Carlson, A., 1979, Appreciation and the natural environment, in *Journal of Aesthetics and Art Criticism*, **37** (3): 267-75.

Carlson, A., 1990, Whose vision? Whose meanings? Whose values? Pluralism and objectivity in landscape analysis, in P. Groth, ed., *Vision, culture, and landscape: working papers from the Berkeley symposium on cultural landscape interpretation*, Department of Landscape Architecture, University of California, Berkeley.

Carter, C.L., 1976, Aesthetic values and human habitation: a philosophical and interdisciplinary approach to environmental aesthetics, in P. Bearse *et al.*, eds., *American values and habitat: a research agenda*, American Association for the Advancement of Science, Washington, DC.

Caruana, W., ed., 1989, *Windows on the dreaming: Aboriginal paintings in the Australian National Gallery*, Australian National Gallery/Ellsyd Press, Chippendale, NSW.

Cassirer, E., 1944, *An essay on man: an introduction to a philosophy of human culture*, Yale University Press, New Haven, Ct.

Chatwin, B., 1987, *The songlines*, Jonathan Cape, London.

Clamp, P., Powell, M., 1982, Prospect-refuge theory under test, in *Landscape Research*, **7** (Winter): 7-8.

Collingwood, R., 1938, *The principles of art*, Oxford University Press.

Colquhoun, A., 1982, *Essays in architectural criticism: modern architecture and historical change*, MIT Press, Cambridge, Mass.

Cooper, C., 1974, The house as a symbol of self, in J. Lang *et al.*, eds., *Designing for human behavior: architecture and the behavioral sciences*, Dowden, Hutchinson and Ross, Stroudsburg, Pa.

Cosgrove, D., 1984, *Social formation and symbolic landscape*, Barnes and Noble, Totowa, NJ.

Cosgrove, D., 1989, Geography is everywhere: culture and symbolism in human landscapes, in D. Gregory and R. Walford, eds., *Horizons in human geography*, Barnes and Noble, Totowa, NJ.

Cosgrove, D., 1990, Spectacle and society: landscape as theater in pre-modern and post-modern cities, in P. Groth, ed., *Vision, culture, and landscape: working papers from the Berkeley symposium on cultural landscape interpretation*, Department of Landscape Architecture, University of California, Berkeley.

Costonis, J.J., 1982, Law and aesthetics: a critique and a reformulation of the dilemmas, in *Michigan Law Review*, **80** (3): 355-461.

Costonis, J.J., 1989, *Icons and aliens: law, aesthetics, and environmental change*, University of Illinois Press, Urbana.

Coughlin, R.E., Goldstein, K.A., 1970, *The extent of agreement among observers on environmental attractiveness*, RSRI Discussion Paper Series No. 37, Regional Science Research Institute, Philadelphia.

Craik, K.H., 1970, The environmental dispositions of environmental decision-makers, in *Annals of the American Academy of Political and Social Science*, **389** (May): 87-94.

Craik, K.H., 1972, Appraising the objectivity of landscape dimensions, in J.V. Krutilla, ed., *Natural environments: studies in theoretical and applied analysis*, Resources for the Future, Washington, DC.

Craik, K.H., 1975, Individual variations in landscape description, in E.H. Zube, R.O. Brush, and J.Gy. Fabos, eds., *Landscape assessment: values, perceptions and resources*, Dowden, Hutchinson and Ross, Stroudsburg, Pa.

Craik, K.H., 1986, Psychological reflections on landscape, in E.C. Penning-Rowsell and D. Lowenthal, eds., *Landscape meanings and values*, Allen and Unwin, London.

Crawford, D.W., 1976, Review of *The experience of landscape*, by Jay Appleton, in *Journal of Aesthetics and Art Criticism*, **34** (3): 367-9.

Croce, B., 1961 [1913], *The breviary of aesthetic*, trans. D. Ainslie, Rice Institute Pamphlet, Vol. 47, No. 4, Houston, Texas.

Cullen, G., 1961, *Townscape*, Architectural Press, London.

Daniel, H., ed., 1989, *Expressway*, Penguin, Ringwood, Vic.

Daniel, T.C., Boster, R.S., 1976, *Measuring landscape esthetics: the Scenic Beauty Estimation Method*, USDA Forest Service Research Paper RM-167, Rocky Mountain Forest and Range Experiment Station, Fort Collins, Co.

Daniel, T.C., Schroeder, H., 1979, Scenic Beauty Estimation Model: predicting perceived beauty of forest landscapes, in *Proceedings of Our National Landscape: a conference on applied techniques for analysis and management of the visual resource*, USDA Forest Service General Technical Report PSW-35, Pacific Southwest Forest and Range Experiment Station, Berkeley, Ca.

Danto, A., 1964, The artworld, in *Journal of Philosophy*, **61** (17): 571-84.

Dear, M.J., 1986, Postmodernism and planning, in *Environment and Planning D: Society and Space*, **4** (3): 367-84.

Dearden, P., 1984, Factors influencing landscape preferences: an empirical investigation, in *Landscape Planning*, **11** (4): 293-306.

Dearden, P., 1989, Societal landscape preferences: a pyramid of influences, in P. Dearden and B. Sadler, eds., *Landscape evaluation: approaches and applications*, Western Geographical Series Vol. 25, Department of Geography, University of Victoria, Victoria, BC.

Dewey, J., 1929, *Experience and nature*, George Allen and Unwin, London.

Dewey, J., 1934, *Art as experience*, Minton, Balch, New York.

Dubos, R., 1976, Symbiosis between the earth and humankind, in *Science*, **193** (4252): 459-62.

Duncan, J.S., 1973, Landscape taste as a symbol of group identity: a Westchester County village, in *Geographical Review*, **63** (3): 334-55.

Eaton, M.M., 1989, *Aesthetics and the good life*, Associated University Presses, Cranbury, NJ.

Eliot, T.S., 1957, Traditional and the individual talent, in *The sacred wood: essays in poetry and criticism*, Methuen, London.

Ellenberger, H.F., 1958, A clinical introduction to psychiatric phenomenology and existential analysis, in R. May, E. Angel and H.F. Ellenberger, eds., *Existence: a new dimension in psychiatry and psychology*, Basic Books, New York.

Fines, K.D., 1968, Landscape evaluation: a research project in East Sussex, in *Regional Studies*, **2** (1): 41-55.

Foglietta, T.M., 1983, Why 17th and Locust should be saved, in *Welcomat* [Philadelphia] (January 5): 8.

Forrest, J., 1988, *Lord I'm coming home: everyday aesthetics in Tidewater North Carolina*, Cornell University Press, Ithaca, NY.

Foster, H., 1985, Postmodernism: a preface, in H. Foster, ed., *Postmodern culture*, Pluto Press, London.

Frampton, K., 1982, *Modern architecture and the critical present*, Architectural Design and Academy Editions, New York.

Frampton, K., 1985, Towards a critical regionalism: six points for an architecture of resistance, in H. Foster, ed., *Postmodern culture*, Pluto Press, London.

Frey, R., 1983, How haste made waste: three buildings saved - at what cost? in *Welcomat* [Philadelphia] (January 19): 1.

Fuller, P., 1986, *The Australian scapegoat: towards an antipodean aesthetic*, University of Western Australia Press, Perth.

Gadamer, H.-G., 1975, *Truth and method*, Crossroad, New York.

Ganem, M., 1987, Master planner Alexander Cooper: building cities from scratch, in *M* (March): 69-75.

Gans, H.J., 1962, *The urban villagers: group and class in the life of Italian-Americans*, Free Press, New York.

Gans, H.J., 1968, *People and plans: essays on urban problems and solutions*, Basic Books, New York.

Gimblett, H.R., Itami, R.M., Fitzgibbon, J.E., 1985, Mystery in an information processing model of landscape preference, in *Landscape Journal*, **4** (2): 87-95.

Giurgola, R., 1987, Architecture: more than a building, in *Architecture Australia*, **76** (3): 43-6.

Gloor, P., 1978, Inputs and outputs of the amygdala: what the amygdala is trying to tell the rest of the brain, in K.E. Livingston and O. Hornykiewicz, eds., *Limbic mechanisms: the continuing evolution of the limbic system concept*, Plenum Press, New York.

Gold, J.R., 1980, *An introduction to behavioural geography*, Oxford University Press.

Goldberger, P., 1987, Where is architecture headed? in *New York Times Magazine* (October 18): 54-8.

Goldberger, P., 1988, A tale of two towers on Boston's Boylston Street, in *New York Times* (January 24): 31-4.

Gombrich, E.H., 1966, The Renaissance theory of art and the rise of landscape, in *Norm and form: studies in the art of the Renaissance*, Phaidon, London.

Gould, S.J., 1980, Sociobiology and the theory of natural selection, in G.W.

Barlow and J. Silverberg, eds., *Sociobiology: beyond nature/nurture?* *Reports, definitions and debate,* AAAS Selected Symposium 35, Westview Press, Boulder, Co.

Greenbie, B.B., 1973, An ethological approach to community design, in W.F.E. Preiser, ed., *Environmental design research, vol. 1: selected papers,* Dowden, Hutchinson and Ross, Stroudsburg, Pa.

Gregory, R.L., 1977, *Eye and brain,* 3rd edn., Weidenfeld and Nicolson, London.

Habermas, J., 1985, Modernity - an incomplete project, in H. Foster, ed., *Postmodern culture,* Pluto Press, London.

Halpern, E., 1983, Letter to the editor, in *Welcomat* [Philadelphia] (February 2): 5.

Hammitt, W.E., 1981, The familiarity-preference component of on-site recreational experiences, in *Leisure Sciences,* **4** (2): 177-93.

Harrison, J., Sarre, P., 1971, Personal construct theory in the measurement of environmental images: problems and methods, in *Environment and Behavior,* **3** (4): 351-74.

Harrison, J., Sarre, P., 1975, Personal construct theory in the measurement of environmental images: applications, in *Environment and Behavior,* **7** (1): 3-58.

Harrison, J., Sarre, P., 1976, Personal construct theory, the repertory grid, and environmental cognition, in G.T. Moore and R.G. Golledge, eds., *Environmental knowing: theories, research, and methods,* Dowden, Hutchinson and Ross, Stroudsburg, Pa.

Harvey, D., 1987, Flexible accumulation through urbanization: reflections on 'postmodernism' in the American city, in *Antipode,* **19** (1/2): 260-86.

Harvey, D., 1989, *The condition of postmodernity,* Basil Blackwell, Oxford.

Hendee, J.C., Harris, R.W., 1970, Foresters' perception of wilderness-user attitudes and preferences, in *Journal of Forestry,* **68** (December): 759-62.

Hepburn, R.W., 1968, Aesthetic appreciation of nature, in H. Osborne, ed., *Aesthetics in the modern world,* Weybright and Talley, New York.

Herzog, T.R., Kaplan, S., Kaplan, R., 1976, The prediction of preference for familiar urban places, in *Environment and Behavior,* **8** (4): 627-45.

Herzog, T.R., Kaplan, S., Kaplan, R., 1982, The prediction of preference for unfamiliar urban places, in *Population and Environment: Behavioral and Social Issues,* **5** (1): 43-59.

Hiss, T., 1987, Reflections: experiencing places, in *The New Yorker* (June 22): 45-68; (June 29): 73-86.

Hiss, T., 1990, *The experience of place,* Knopf, New York.

Hodgson, R.W., Thayer, R.L., 1980, Implied human influence reduces landscape beauty, in *Landscape Planning,* **7** (2): 171-9.

Homans, P., 1979, *Jung in context: modernity and the making of a psychology,* University of Chicago Press.

Hull, D.L., 1980, Sociobiology: another new synthesis, in G.W. Barlow and J. Silverberg, eds., *Sociobiology: beyond nature/nurture? Reports, definitions and debate,* AAAS Selected Symposium 35, Westview Press, Boulder, Co.

Hume, D.A., 1888 [1740], *A treatise of human nature,* ed. L.A. Selby-Bigge, Oxford University Press.

Hume, D.A., 1965 [1757], *Of the standard of taste and other essays,* ed. J.W. Lenz, Bobbs-Merrill, New York.

Humphrey, N.K., 1970, What the frog's eye tells the monkey's brain, in *Brain, Behavior and Evolution,* **3** (4/6): 324-37.

Humphrey, N.K., 1972, Seeing and nothingness, in *New Scientist*, **53** (788): 682-4.

Humphrey, N.K., 1980, Natural aesthetics, in B. Mikellides, ed., *Architecture for people: explorations in a new humane environment*, Holt, Rinehart, Winston, New York.

Huxtable, A.L., 1980, The troubled state of modern architecture, in *New York Review of Books*, **27** (7): 22-9.

Huyssen, A., 1981, The search for tradition: avant-garde and postmodernism in the 1970s, in *New German Critique*, **22** (Winter): 23-40.

Isaac, G., 1980, Casting the net wide: a review of archaeological evidence for early hominid land-use and ecological relations, in L.-K. Königsson, ed., *Current argument on early man*, Pergamon Press, Oxford.

Ittelson, W.H., 1973, Environmental perception and contemporary perceptual theory, in W.H. Ittelson, ed., *Environment and cognition*, Seminar Press, New York.

Izard, C.E., 1984, Emotion-cognition relationships and human development, in C.E. Izard, J. Kagan and R.B. Zajonc, eds., *Emotions, cognition, and behavior*, Cambridge University Press, New York.

Jackson, J.B., 1970, The imitation of nature, in E.H. Zube, ed., *Landscapes: selected writings of J.B. Jackson*, University of Massachusetts Press, Amherst.

Jacobs, A., Appleyard, D., 1987, Toward an urban design manifesto, in *Journal of the American Planning Association*, **53** (1): 112-20.

Jacobs, J., 1961, *The death and life of great American cities*, Random House, New York.

Jacques, D.L., 1980, Landscape appraisal: the case for a subjective theory, in *Journal of Environmental Management*, **10** (2): 107-13.

Jakle, J.A., 1987, *The visual elements of landscape*, University of Massachusetts Press, Amherst.

James, W., 1958 [1899], On a certain blindness in human beings, in *Talks to teachers on psychology: and to students on some of life's ideals*, Norton, New York.

Jeans, D.N., 1977, Review of *The experience of landscape*, by Jay Appleton, in *Australian Geographer*, **13** (5): 345-6.

Jencks, C., 1978, *The language of post-modern architecture*, Academy Editions, London.

Jones, R., 1975, The Neolithic, Paleolithic and the hunting gardeners: man and land in the Antipodes, in R.P. Suggate and M.M. Cresswell, eds., *Quaternary studies: selected papers from the IX International Congress INQUA, 2-10 December 1973*, Bulletin 13, Royal Society of New Zealand, Wellington.

Jung, C.G., 1928, *Contributions to analytical psychology*, Harcourt Brace, New York.

Jung, C.G., 1959, *The archetypes and the collective unconscious*, Pantheon, New York.

Jung, C.G., 1964, *Man and his symbols*, Doubleday, Garden City, NY.

Kanizsa, G., 1979, *Organization in vision: essays on Gestalt perception*, Praeger, New York.

Kant, I., 1911 [1790], *Critique of aesthetic judgement*, trans. J.C. Meredith, Oxford University Press.

Kant, I., 1960 [1764], *Observations on the feeling of the beautiful and sublime*, trans. J.T. Goldthwait, University of California Press, Berkeley.

Kaplan, R., 1973, Predictors of environmental preference: designers and 'clients', in W.F.E. Preiser, ed., *Environmental design research, vol. 1: selected papers*, Dowden, Hutchinson and Ross, Stroudsburg, Pa.

Kaplan, R., 1977, Patterns of environmental preference, in *Environment and Behavior*, **9** (2): 195-216.

Kaplan, R., Herbert, E.J., 1987, Cultural and sub-cultural comparisons in preferences for natural settings, in *Landscape and Urban Planning*, **14** (4): 281-93.

Kaplan, R., Herbert, E.J., 1988, Familiarity and preference: a cross-cultural analysis, in J.L. Nasar, ed., *Environmental aesthetics: theory, research, and applications*, Cambridge University Press.

Kaplan, R., Kaplan, S., 1989, *The experience of nature: a psychological perspective*, Cambridge University Press, New York.

Kaplan, R., Talbot, J.F., 1988, Ethnicity and preference for natural settings: a review and recent findings, in *Landscape and Urban Planning*, **15** (1/2): 107-17.

Kaplan, S., 1972, The challenge of environmental psychology: a proposal for a new functionalism, in *American Psychologist*, **27** (2): 140-3.

Kaplan, S., 1973, Cognitive maps in perception and thought, in R.M. Downs and D. Stea, eds., *Image and environment: cognitive mapping and spatial behavior*, Aldine, Chicago.

Kaplan, S., 1975, An informal model for the prediction of preference, in E.H. Zube, R.O. Brush and J.Gy. Fabos, eds., *Landscape assessment: values, perception and resources*, Dowden, Hutchinson and Ross, Stroudsburg, Pa.

Kaplan, S., 1976, Adaptation, structure, and knowledge, in G.T. Moore and R.G. Golledge, eds., *Environmental knowing: theories, research and methods*, Dowden, Hutchinson and Ross, Stroudsburg, Pa.

Kaplan, S., 1979, Perception and landscape: conceptions and misconceptions, in *Proceedings of Our National Landscape: a conference on applied techniques for analysis and management of the visual resource*, USDA Forest Service General Technical Report PSW-35, Pacific Southwest Forest and Range Experiment Station, Berkeley, Ca.

Kaplan, S., 1987, Aesthetics, affect, and cognition: environmental preference from an evolutionary perspective, in *Environment and Behavior*, **19** (1): 3-32.

Kaplan, S., Kaplan, R., 1989, The visual environment: public participation in design and planning, in *Journal of Social Issues*, **45** (1): 59-86.

Kaplan, S., Kaplan, R., Wendt, J.S., 1972, Rated preference and complexity for natural and urban visual material, in *Perception and Psychophysics*, **12** (4): 354-6.

Keyes, B.E., 1984, Visual preference of a forest trail environment, unpublished master's thesis, University of Tennessee, Knoxville.

Koestler, A., 1964, *The act of creation*, Macmillan, New York.

Köhler, W., 1969, *The task of Gestalt psychology*, Princeton University Press, Princeton, NJ.

Kolb, D., 1990, *Postmodern sophistications: philosophy, architecture, and tradition*, University of Chicago Press.

Kramer, H., 1987, The idea of tradition in American art criticism, in *The American Scholar*, **56** (Summer): 319-27.

Krumholz, N., 1987, Future directions in city planning: a comment, in *Journal of Planning Literature*, **2** (1): 1-6.

Kuhn, T.S., 1970, *The structure of scientific revolutions*, University of Chicago Press.

Kunst-Wilson, W.R. Zajonc, R.B., 1980, Affective discrimination of stimuli

that cannot be recognized, in *Science*, **207** (4430): 557-8.
Kwok, K., 1979, Semantic evaluation of perceived environment: a cross-cultural replication, in *Man-Environment Systems*, **9** (5): 243-9.
Lang, J., 1987, *Creating architectural theory: the role of the behavioral sciences in environmental design*, Van Nostrand Reinhold, New York.
Langer, S.K., 1953, *Feeling and form: a theory of art*, Scribner's, New York.
Lazarus, R.S., 1982, Thoughts on the relations between emotion and cognition, in *American Psychologist*, **37** (9): 1019-24.
Lazarus, R.S., 1984, On the primacy of cognition, in *American Psychologist*, **39** (2): 124-9.
Le Corbusier, 1964, *La ville radieuse*, Vincent, Fréal, Paris.
Leff, H.L., Gordon, L.R., 1979, Environmental cognitive sets: a longitudinal study, in *Environment and Behavior*, **11** (3): 291-327.
Leff, H.L., Gordon, L.R., Ferguson, J.G., 1974, Cognitive set and environmental awareness, in *Environment and Behavior*, **6** (4): 395-447.
Levi, D., 1974, The Gestalt psychology of expression in architecture, in J. Lang *et al.*, eds., *Designing for human behavior: architecture and the behavioral sciences*, Dowden, Hutchinson and Ross, Stroudsburg, Pa.
Lewis, P.F., 1973, The geographer as landscape critic, in P.F. Lewis, D. Lowenthal and Y.-F. Tuan, *Visual blight in America*, Commission on College Geography Resource Paper No. 23, Association of American Geographers, Washington, DC.
Lipman, A., 1969, The architectural belief system and social behavior, in *British Journal of Sociology*, **20** (2): 190-204.
Little, B.R., 1975, Specialization and the varieties of environmental experience: empirical studies within the personality paradigm, in S. Wapner, S.B. Cohen and B. Kaplan, eds., *Experiencing the environment*, Plenum Press, New York.
Livingstone, F.B., 1980, Cultural causes of genetic change, in G.W. Barlow and J. Silverberg, eds., *Sociobiology: beyond nature/nurture? Reports, definitions and debate*, AAAS Selected Symposium 35, Westview Press, Boulder, Co.
Lohr, S., 1987, That prince and his city: critic or pain? in *New York Times* (December 6): 7.
Lowenthal, D., 1962-3, Not every prospect pleases, in *Landscape*, **12** (2): 19-23.
Lynch, K., 1976, *Managing the sense of a region*, MIT Press, Cambridge, Mass.
Lyons, E., 1983, Demographic correlates of landscape preference, in *Environment and Behavior*, **15** (4): 487-511.
Lyotard, J.-F., 1984, *The postmodern condition: a report on knowledge*, University of Minnesota Press, Minneapolis.
MacCannell, D., 1976, *The tourist: a new theory of the leisure class*, Macmillan, London.
Maciá, A., 1979, Visual perception of landscape: sex and personality differences, in G.H. Elsner and R.C. Smardon, eds., *Proceedings of Our National Landscape: a conference on applied techniques for analysis and management of the visual resource*, USDA Forest Service Technical Report PSW-35, Pacific Southwest Forest and Range Experiment Station, Berkeley, Ca.
McKechnie, G., 1970, Measuring environmental dispositions with the Environmental Response Inventory, in J. Archea and C. Eastman, eds.,

*EDRA two: proceedings of the Second Annual Environmental Design Research Association Conference*, Dowden, Hutchinson and Ross, Stroudsburg, Pa.

MacKinnon, D.W., 1962, The nature and nurture of creative talent, in *American Psychologist*, **17** (7): 484-95.

MacLean, P.D., 1958a, Contrasting functions of limbic and neocortical systems of the brain and their relevance to psychophysiological aspects of medicine, in *American Journal of Medicine*, **25** (5): 611-26.

MacLean, P.D., 1958b, The limbic system with respect to self-preservation and the preservation of the species, in *Journal of Nervous and Mental Disease*, **127** (1): 1-11.

MacLean, P.D., 1959, The limbic system with respect to two basic life principles, in M.A.B. Brazier, ed., *The central nervous system and behavior*, Josiah Macy Jr. Foundation, New York.

MacLean, P.D., 1962, New findings relevant to the evolution of the psychosexual functions of the brain, in *Journal of Nervous and Mental Disease*, **135** (4): 289-301.

MacLean, P.D., 1973a, The brain's generation gap: some human implications, in *Zygon: Journal of Religion and Science*, **8** (2): 113-27.

MacLean, P.D., 1973b, Man's limbic brain and the psychoses, in T.J. Boag and D. Campbell, eds., *A triune concept of brain and behaviour*, University of Toronto Press.

MacLean, P.D., 1973c, Man's reptilian and limbic inheritance, in T.J. Boag and D. Campbell, eds., *A triune concept of brain and behaviour*, University of Toronto Press.

MacLean, P.D., 1973d, New trends in man's evolution, in T.J. Boag and D. Campbell, eds., *A triune concept of brain and behaviour*, University of Toronto Press.

Margolis, J., 1977, The ontological peculiarity of works of art, in *Journal of Aesthetics and Art Criticism*, **36** (1): 45-50.

May, R., 1958a, Contributions of existential psychotherapy, in R. May, E. Angel and H.F. Ellenberger, eds., *Existence: a new dimension in psychiatry and psychology*, Basic Books, New York.

May, R., 1958b, The origins and significance of the existential movement in psychology, in R. May, E. Angel and H.F. Ellenberger, eds., *Existence: a new dimension in psychiatry and psychology*, Basic Books, New York.

Merquior, J.G., 1979, Remarks on the theory of culture, in *The veil and the mask: essays on culture and ideology*, Routledge and Kegan Paul, London.

Meyer, L.B., 1979, Toward a theory of style, in B. Lang, ed., *The concept of style*, University of Pennsylvania Press, Philadelphia.

Midgley, M., 1978, *Beast and man: the roots of human nature*, The Harvester Press, Hassocks, UK.

Moore, R.Y., 1973, Retinohypothalamic projection in mammals: a comparative study, in *Brain Research*, **49** (2): 403-9.

Moreland, R.L., Zajonc, R.B., 1977, Is stimulus recognition a necessary condition for the occurrence of exposure effects? in *Journal of Personality and Social Psychology*, **35** (4): 191-9.

Mumford, L., 1952, *Art and technics*, Columbia University Press, New York.

Mumford, L., 1962, The case against 'modern architecture', in *Architectural Record*, **131** (April): 155-62.

Nasar, J.L., 1980, Influence of familiarity on responses to visual qualities of neighborhoods, in *Perceptual and Motor Skills*, **51** (2): 635-42.

Nasar, J.L., 1984, Visual preferences in urban street scenes: a cross-cultural comparison between Japan and the United States, in *Journal of Cross-Cultural Psychology*, **15** (1): 79-93.

Nasar, J.L., et al., 1988, The emotional quality of scenes and observation points: a look at prospect and refuge, in J.L. Nasar, ed., *Environmental aesthetics: theory, research, and applications*, Cambridge University Press.

Neutze, M., 1988, *Planning as urban management: a critical assessment*, Urban Research Unit Working Paper Series No. 6, Research School of Social Sciences, The Australian National University, Canberra.

Nicholson, M.H., 1962, *Mountain gloom and mountain glory: the development of the aesthetics of the infinite*, Norton, New York.

Orians, G.H., 1980, Habitat selection: general theory and applications to human behavior, in J.S. Lockard, ed., *The evolution of human social behavior*, Elsevier, New York.

Orians, G.H., 1986, An ecological and evolutionary approach to landscape aesthetics, in E.C. Penning-Rowsell and D. Lowenthal, eds., *Landscape meanings and values*, Allen and Unwin, London.

Paillard, J., Michel, F., Stelmach, G., 1983, Localization without content: a tactile analogue of 'blind sight', in *Archives of Neurology*, **40** (9): 548-51.

Passmore, J.A., 1967, The dreariness of aesthetics, in W. Elton, ed., *Aesthetics and language*, Basil Blackwell, Oxford.

Peattie, L., 1969, Conflicting views of the project: Caracas versus the site, in L. Rodwin, ed., *Planning urban growth and development: the experience of the Guayana program of Venezuela*, MIT Press, Cambridge, Mass.

Peattie, L., 1987, *Planning: rethinking Ciudad Guayana*, University of Michigan Press, Ann Arbor.

Pedersen, D.M., 1978a, Dimensions of environmental perception, in *Multivariate Experimental Clinical Research*, **3** (5): 209-18.

Pedersen, D.M., 1978b, The relationship between environmental familiarity and environmental preference, in *Perceptual and Motor Skills*, **47** (3): 739-43.

Penning-Rowsell, E.C., 1981, Fluctuating fortunes in gauging landscape value, in *Progress in Human Geography*, **5** (1): 25-41.

Peterson, S.K., 1980, Space and anti-space, in *Harvard Architectural Review: beyond the modern movement*, MIT Press, Cambridge, Mass.

Plato, 1937, *The dialogues of Plato*, trans. B. Jowett, Random House, New York.

Plato, 1969, Phaedo, in *The last days of Socrates*, trans. H. Tredennick, Penguin Books, Harmondsworth, UK.

Porteous, J.D., 1982a, Approaches to environmental aesthetics, in *Journal of Environmental Psychology*, **2** (1): 53-66.

Porteous, J.D., 1982b, Urban environmental aesthetics, in B. Sadler and A. Carlson, eds., *Environmental aesthetics: essays in interpretation*, Western Geographical Series Vol. 20, Department of Geography, University of Victoria, Victoria, BC.

Porteous, J.D., 1985, Smellscape, in *Progress in Human Geography*, **9** (3): 356-78.

Porteous, J.D., Mastin, J.F., 1985, Soundscape, in *Journal of Architectural and Planning Research*, **2** (3): 169-86.

Porter, M.V., 1987, The role of spatial quality and familiarity in determining countryside landscape preference, unpublished master's thesis, University of Washington, Seattle.

Priestley, T., 1983, The field of visual analysis and resource management: a bibliographic analysis and perspective, in *Landscape Journal*, 2 (2): 52-9.

Punter, J.V., 1982, Landscape aesthetics: a synthesis and critique, in J.R. Gold and J. Burgess, eds., *Valued environments*, George Allen and Unwin, London.

Rabinowitz, C.B., Coughlin, R.E., 1970, *Analysis of landscape characteristics relevant to preference*, RSRI Discussion Paper Series No. 38, Regional Science Research Institute, Philadelphia.

Rappaport, R.A., 1986, Desecrating the holy woman: Derek Freeman's attack on Margaret Mead, in *The American Scholar*, 55 (Summer): 313-47.

Relph, E., 1976, *Place and placelessness*, Pion, London.

Rodie, S.N., 1985, Visual quality perceptions in the Flint Hills: assessing the effects of cultural modifications, unpublished master's thesis, Kansas State University, Manhattan.

Rose, M.C., 1976, Nature as aesthetic object: an essay in meta-aesthetics, in *British Journal of Aesthetics*, 16 (1): 3-12.

Rowntree, L.B., 1981, Creating a sense of place: the evolution of historic preservation of Salzburg, Austria, in *Journal of Urban History*, 8 (1): 61-76.

Rowntree, L.B., Conkey, M.W., 1980, Symbolism and the cultural landscape, in *Annals of the Association of American Geographers*, 70 (4): 459-74.

Sancar, F.H., 1985, Towards theory generation in landscape aesthetics, in *Landscape Journal*, 4 (2): 116-23.

Sancar, F.H., 1989, A critique of criticism: can the avant garde embrace the entire landscape? in *Avant Garde: Journal of Theory and Criticism in Architecture and the Arts*, 2 (Summer): 78-91.

Santayana, G., 1961 [1896], *The sense of beauty: being the outline of aesthetic theory*, Collier Books, New York.

Sauer, C.O., 1963, The morphology of landscape, in J. Leighly, ed., *Land and life: a selection from the writings of Carl Ortwin Sauer*, University of California Press, Berkeley.

Schafer, R.M., 1977, *The tuning of the world: toward a theory of soundscape design*, Knopf, New York.

Schafer, R.M., 1985, Acoustic space, in D. Seamon and R. Mugerauer, eds., *Dwelling, place and environment: towards a phenomenology of person and world*, Martinus Nijhoff, Dordrecht.

Schauman, S., 1988a, Countryside scenic assessment: tools and an application, in *Landscape and Urban Planning*, 15 (3/4): 227-39.

Schauman, S., 1988b, Scenic value of countryside landscapes to local residents: a Whatcom County, Washington, case study, in *Landscape Journal*, 7 (1): 40-56.

Schauman, S., Pfender, M., 1982, *An assessment procedure for countryside landscapes*, Department of Landscape Architecture, University of Washington, Seattle.

Scribner, S., 1985, Vygotsky's uses of history, in J.V. Wertsch, ed., *Culture, communication, and cognition: Vygotskian perspectives*, Cambridge University Press.

Scruton, R., 1974, *Art and imagination: a study in the philosophy of mind*, Methuen, London.

Scruton, R., 1979, *The aesthetics of architecture*, Princeton University Press, Princeton, NJ.

Seamon, D., 1982, The phenomenological contribution to environmental psychology, in *Journal of Environmental Psychology*, 2 (2): 119-40.

Seamon, J.G., Brody, N., Kauff, D.M., 1983a, Affective discrimination of stimuli that are not recognized: effects of shadowing, masking, and cerebral laterality, in *Journal of Experimental Psychology: Learning, Memory, and Cognition*, **9** (3): 544-55.

Seamon, J.G., Brody, N., Kauff, D.M., 1983b, Affective discrimination of stimuli that are not recognized, II: effect of delay between study and test, in *Bulletin of the Psychonomic Society*, **21** (3): 187-9.

Seamon, J.G., Marsh, R.L., Brody, N., 1984, Critical importance of exposure duration for affective discrimination of stimuli that are not recognized, in *Journal of Experimental Psychology: Learning, Memory, and Cognition*, **10** (3): 465-9.

Sell, J.L., Taylor, J.G., Zube, E.H., 1984, Toward a theoretical framework for landscape perception, in T.F. Saarinen, D. Seamon and J.L. Sell, eds., *Environmental perception and behavior: an inventory and prospect*, Research Paper No. 209, Department of Geography, University of Chicago.

Shafer, E.L., Brush, R.O., 1977, How to measure preferences for photographs of natural landscapes, in *Landscape Planning*, **4** (3): 237-56.

Shafer, E.L., Hamilton, J.F., Schmidt, E.A., 1969, Natural landscape preferences: a predictive model, in *Journal of Leisure Research*, **1** (1): 1-9.

Shafer, E.L., Mietz, J., 1970, *It seems possible to quantify scenic beauty in photographs*, USDA Forest Service Research Paper NE-162, USDA Northeastern Forest Experiment Station, Upper Darby, Pa.

Shafer, E.L., Tooby, M., 1973, Landscape preferences: an international replication, in *Journal of Leisure Research*, **5** (3): 60-5.

Shepard, P., 1967, *Man in the landscape: a historic view of the esthetics of nature*, Knopf, New York.

Shepard, P., 1969, *English reaction to the New Zealand landscape before 1850*, Pacific Viewpoint Monograph No. 4, Department of Geography, Victoria University of Wellington, NZ.

Sheppard, A., 1987, *Aesthetics: an introduction to the philosophy of art*, Oxford University Press.

Silverberg, J., 1980, Sociobiology, the new synthesis? An anthropologist's perspective, in G.W. Barlow and J. Silverberg, eds., *Sociobiology: beyond nature/nurture? Reports, definitions and debate*, AAAS Selected Symposium 35, Westview Press, Boulder, Co.

Smith, B., 1979, *Place, taste, and tradition: a study of Australian art since 1788*, Oxford University Press, Melbourne.

Smith, B., 1989, *European vision and the South Pacific*, 2nd edn., Oxford University Press, Melbourne.

Smith, P.F., 1977, *The syntax of cities*, Hutchinson, London.

Sonnenfeld, J., 1966, Variable values in space and landscape: an inquiry into the nature of environmental necessity, in *Journal of Social Issues*, **22** (4): 71-82.

Sonnenfeld, J., 1969, Equivalence and distortion of the perceptual environment, in *Environment and Behavior*, **1** (1): 83-99.

Southworth, M., 1969, The sonic environment of cities, in *Environment and Behavior*, **1** (1): 49-70.

Sparshott, F.E., 1972, Figuring the ground: notes on some theoretical problems of the aesthetic environment, in *Journal of Aesthetic Education*, **6** (3): 11-23.

Stern, R., 1977, At the edge of post-modernism: some methods, paradigms and principles for architecture at the end of the modern movement, in *Architectural Design*, **47** (4): 275-86.

Stolnitz, J., 1960, *Aesthetics and the philosophy of art criticism: a critical introduction*, Houghton Mifflin, Boston.

Stolnitz, J., 1961, On the origins of 'aesthetic disinterestedness', in *Journal of Aesthetics and Art Criticism*, **20** (2): 131-43.

Tips, W.E.J., Savasdisara, T., 1986a, The influence of the environmental background of subjects on their landscape preference evaluation, in *Landscape and Urban Planning*, **13** (2): 125-33.

Tips, W.E.J., Savasdisara, T., 1986b, Landscape preference evaluation and sociocultural background: a comparison among Asian countries, in *Journal of Environmental Management*, **22** (2): 113-24.

Tolstoy, L., 1955 [1896], *What is art?* and essays on art, trans. A. Maude, Oxford University Press.

Tomkins, S.S., 1981, The quest for primary motives: biography and autobiography of an idea, in *Journal of Personality and Social Psychology*, **41** (2): 306-29.

Toulmin, S., 1978, The Mozart of psychology, in *New York Review of Books*, **25** (14): 51-7.

Trancik, R., 1986, *Finding lost space: theories of urban design*, Van Nostrand Reinhold, New York.

Tuan, Y.-F., 1971a, Geography, phenomenology, and the study of human nature, in *Canadian Geographer*, **15** (3): 181-92.

Tuan, Y.-F., 1971b, *Man and nature*, Commission on College Geography Resource Paper No. 10, Association of American Geographers, Washington, DC.

Tuan, Y.-F., 1974, *Topophilia: a study of environmental perception, attitudes, and values*, Prentice-Hall, Englewood Cliffs, NJ.

Tuan, Y.-F., 1976a, Humanistic geography, in *Annals of the Association of American Geographers*, **66** (2): 266-76.

Tuan, Y.-F., 1976b, Review of *The experience of landscape*, by Jay Appleton, in *Professional Geographer*, **28** (1): 104-5.

Tuan, Y.-F., 1989, Surface phenomena and aesthetic experience, in *Annals of the Association of American Geographers*, **79** (2): 233-41.

Tunnard, C., 1978, *A world with a view: an inquiry into the nature of scenic values*, Yale University Press, New Haven, Ct.

Twight, B.W., Catton, W.R., 1975, The politics of images: forest managers vs. recreation publics, in *Natural Resources Journal*, **15** (2): 297-306.

Tyng, A.G., 1969, Geometric expansions of consciousness, in *Zodiac*, **19** (1): 130-62.

Tzonis, A., Lefaivre, L., 1981, The grid and the pathway: an introduction to the work of Dimitris and Susana Antonakakis, in *Architecture in Greece*, **15** (2): 164-78.

Ulrich, R.S., 1977, Visual landscape preference: a model and application, in *Man-Environment Systems*, **7** (5): 279-93.

Ulrich, R.S., 1979, Visual landscapes and psychological well-being, in *Landscape Research*, **4** (1): 17-23.

Ulrich, R.S., 1981, Natural versus urban scenes: some psychophysiological effects, in *Environment and Behavior*, **13** (5): 523-56.

Ulrich, R.S., 1983, Aesthetic and affective response to natural environment, in I. Altman and J.F. Wohlwill, eds., *Behavior and the natural environment*, Plenum Press, New York.

Ulrich, R.S., 1986, Human responses to vegetation and landscapes, in *Landscape and Urban Planning*, **13** (1): 29-44.

Underhill, N., 1987, William Robinson, *The ID Show*, University of Tasmania, Hobart.

Unwin, K.I., 1975, The relationship of observer and landscape in landscape evaluation, in *Transactions of the Institute of British Geographers*, **66**: 130-4.

Urmson, J.O., 1957, What makes a situation aesthetic? in *Proceedings of the Aristotelian Society*, **31** (Supplement): 75-92.

Van den Berg, J.H., 1955, *The phenomenological approach to psychiatry: an introduction to recent phenomenological psychopathology*, Charles C. Thomas, Springfield, Ill.

Venturi, R., 1966, *Complexity and contradiction in architecture*, Museum of Modern Art, New York.

Venturi, R., Scott Brown, D., Izenour, S., 1977, *Learning from Las Vegas*, MIT Press, Cambridge, Mass.

Von der Heydt, R., Peterhans, E., Baumgartner, G., 1984, Illusory contours and cortical neuron responses, in *Science*, **224** (4654): 1260-2.

Vygotsky, L.S., 1978, *Mind in society: the development of higher psychological processes*, M. Cole *et al.*, eds., Harvard University Press, Cambridge, Mass.

Vygotsky, L.S., 1981a [1929], The development of higher forms of attention, in J.V. Wertsch, ed., *The concept of activity in Soviet psychology*, Sharpe, Armonk, NY.

Vygotsky, L.S., 1981b [1960], The genesis of higher mental functions, in J.V. Wertsch, ed., *The concept of activity in Soviet psychology*, Sharpe, Armonk, NY.

Vygotsky, L.S., 1981c [1960], The instrumental method in psychology, in J.V. Wertsch, ed., *The concept of activity in Soviet psychology*, Sharpe, Armonk, NY.

Webber, M.M., 1964, The urban place and the nonplace urban realm, in M.M. Webber, *et al.*, eds., *Explorations into urban structure*, University of Pennsylvania Press, Philadelphia.

Weinstein, N.D., 1976, The statistical prediction of environmental preferences: problems of validity and application, in *Environment and Behavior*, **8** (4): 611-26.

Weirick, J., 1989, Don't you believe it: critical response to the *New Parliament House*, in *Transition*, **27/28** (Summer/Autumn): 7-66.

Weiskrantz, L., 1986, *Blindsight: a case study and implications*, Oxford University Press.

Weiskrantz, L., 1987, Brain function and awareness, in R.L. Gregory, ed., *The Oxford companion to the mind*, Oxford University Press.

Weitz, M., 1956, The role of theory in aesthetics, in *Journal of Aesthetics and Art Criticism*, **15** (1): 27-35.

Wellman, J.D., Buhyoff, G.J., 1980, Effects of regional familiarity on landscape preferences, in *Journal of Environmental Management*, **11** (2): 105-10.

Wertsch, J.V., 1985, *Vygotsky and the social formation of mind*, Harvard University Press, Cambridge, Mass.

Wilde, O., 1927, The decay of lying, in *The best known works of Oscar Wilde*, Blue Ribbon Books, New York.

Wilson, E.O., 1975, *Sociobiology: the new synthesis*, Harvard University Press, Cambridge, Mass.

Wilson, E.O., 1984, *Biophilia*, Harvard University Press, Cambridge, Mass.

Wilson, J.P., 1987, Indulging a passion for piazzas, in *New York Times* (November 22): 41.

Wilson, W.R., 1979, Feeling more than we can know: exposure effects without learning, in *Journal of Personality and Social Psychology*, **37** (6): 811-21.

Wohlwill, J.F., 1968, Amount of stimulus exploration and preference as differential functions of stimulus complexity, in *Perception and Psychophysics*, **4** (5): 307-12.

Wohlwill, J.F., 1976, Environmental aesthetics: the environment as a source of affect, in I. Altman and J.F. Wohlwill, eds., *Human behavior and environment: advances in theory and research*, Vol. 1, Plenum Press, New York.

Wohlwill, J.F., 1983, The concept of nature: a psychologist's view, in I. Altman and J.F. Wohlwill, eds., *Behavior and the natural environment*, Plenum Press, New York.

Wolfe, T., 1981, *From Bauhaus to our house*, Farrar Straus Giroux, New York.

Woodcock, D.M., 1982, A functionalist approach to environmental preference, unpublished Ph.D. dissertation, University of Michigan, Ann Arbor.

Yang, B., 1988, A cross-cultural comparison of preference for Korean, Japanese, and Western landscape styles, unpublished Ph.D. dissertation, University of Michigan, Ann Arbor.

Zajonc, R.B., 1980, Feeling and thinking: preferences need no inferences, in *American Psychologist*, **35** (2): 151-75.

Zajonc, R.B., 1981, A one-factor mind about mind and emotion, in *American Psychologist*, **36** (1): 102-3.

Zajonc, R.B., 1984, On the primacy of affect, in *American Psychologist*, **39** (2): 117-23.

Zube, E.H., 1974, Cross-disciplinary and intermode agreement on the description and evaluation of landscape resources, in *Environment and Behavior*, **6** (1): 69-89.

Zube, E.H., 1984, Themes in landscape assessment theory, in *Landscape Journal*, **3** (2): 104-10.

Zube, E.H., Mills, L.V., 1976, Cross-cultural explorations in landscape perception, in E.H. Zube, ed., *Studies in landscape perception*, Institute for Man and Environment Publication No. R-76-1, University of Massachusetts, Amherst.

Zube, E.H., Pitt, D.G., 1981, Cross-cultural perceptions of scenic and heritage landscapes, in *Landscape Planning*, **8** (1): 69-87.

Zube, E.H., Pitt, D.G., Anderson, T.W., 1975, Perception and prediction of scenic resource values of the Northeast, in E.H. Zube, R.O. Brush and J.Gy. Fabos, eds., *Landscape assessment: values, perceptions and resources*, Dowden, Hutchinson and Ross, Stroudsburg, Pa.

Zube, E.H., Sell, J.L., Taylor, J.G., 1982, Landscape perception: research, application and theory, in *Landscape Planning*, **9** (1): 1-33.

# INDEX

Note: Numerals in *italics* are page numbers of plates.